I KNEW YOU
WERE THERE

I KNEW YOU
WERE THERE

A Stolen Child's Search for Her Irish Mother

MARIE O'LEARY WYDRA &
MEGAN (WYDRA) McKERCHER

SHAMROCK
PUBLISHING

SHAMROCK
PUBLISHING

I had two beautiful and healthy babies—a daughter and a son. Yet my heart yearned for another. My husband and I didn't know if we could afford it, though. I was already working one, sometimes two jobs, and he picked up as much overtime as he could.

I found a way. After I put out the word that I was looking for some side work and why, a hospital pharmacist, Andy Tang, whom I worked with, hired me to teach English to his niece and nephew, newly arrived from China. That extra money got my husband on board.

The day we were blessed with our third child, Megan, Andy visited us in the delivery room. I was beaming and holding her up to my face, and I'll never forget his words and mine. He said, "Are you happy?" I replied, "I am now!"

So many angels like him showed up in my life to guide me on my journey, which wasn't easy. Without them, I would not have found the comfort and joy that my life had in store. I'm forever grateful to them; they'll never know just how much I needed them.

CONTENTS

About the Authors   ix

Prelude   xi

Introduction   xiii

PART I
Surviving by Growing Up Too Soon

Chapter 1   *1*

Chapter 2   *17*

Chapter 3   *27*

Chapter 4   *43*

PART II
The Quest

Chapter 5   *57*

Chapter 6   *71*

Chapter 7   *85*

Chapter 8   *117*

Resources   127

Acknowledgments   129

ABOUT THE AUTHORS

An entrepreneur, MEGAN McKERCHER owns and operates Heart & Home, a residential care facility, which she founded upon graduation from college. Every chance she gets, she and her husband love to travel with their family. She considers her son to be her greatest accomplishment and joy.

Overcoming her difficult childhood, MARIE WYDRA has dedicated her life to caring for people, from the very youngest to the very oldest. She hopes her story will inspire others to overcome their own hardships. She is proudest of her nursing career of more than forty years and her three beautiful children and five gorgeous grandchildren.

PRELUDE

MY JOURNEY
TO THE
UNITED STATES

I was an adult before my adoptive father, Joe, told me what little he'd learned from the Aer Lingus flight attendant who chaperoned two-year-old me on my flight from Ireland to the US in 1956. I've often imagined what that trip was like from her perspective:

It's funny how you can easily recall seemingly insignificant occurrences in your life as time passes by. I had been a flight attendant for about a year when I was assigned to escort a little girl traveling to the US to be adopted.

As I awaited her arrival, I wondered what her life had been like in a mother and baby home. I had heard stories of abuse and cruelty. Months after a schoolmate of mine had been whisked off in the night to one of them, she seemed so haunted when she returned. But even in our small village where everyone knew everything about everyone, no words about her experience were ever spoken.

Before long, up stepped a prim and proper-looking social worker who seemed as impatient to unload her charge as the little one was to squirm away. The woman handed her off to me, saying, "Good luck with this one! You'll have your hands full. Her name is Maria O'Leary, and she never stops fidgeting. And that bandage on her nose? A little boy at the orphanage smacked her with his shoe when she tried to steal his food." With that, the social worker handed me paperwork and the satchel of the child's belongings, and off she went without even a backward glance.

I knelt to say hello to Maria, a sight to behold with her little bandaged nose and crooked fringe. As her big blue-green eyes shyly met mine, she smiled. She willingly accepted my hand, and together we boarded the plane. Then she climbed up on the seat and stared out of the window as if she was saying goodbye.

Maria seemed curious about this new adventure and the people who walked past our row. She was quiet, the opposite of the whirlwind the woman had described. When I sang to her, her eyes lit up and she tried to sing along. She fell asleep as I held her hand and thought how lucky she was to be getting a family who wanted a child and would give her the love that she most certainly deserved.

When we landed in New York, I felt a tug at my heart at the thought of saying goodbye. Maria let me give her a hug, and as our eyes met for the last time, I hoped that she would have a happy childhood like my own. Then I silently prayed, "God, please let angels go with her to her new home." I hope they did!

INTRODUCTION

In Ireland in the fifties, becoming pregnant out of wedlock was considered a mortal sin committed by the whole family. Many priests who found out that an unwed girl in their parish was pregnant would abduct her from her home in the middle of the night, take her to a mother and baby home to have the child, and ban the rest of the family from taking communion.

The reflected shame of an unwed mother was so great that sometimes the families themselves abducted the girls to these homes. The stories came out only under a cloud of secrecy and were never spoken of again.

The nuns who ran these homes cruelly shamed and mistreated those poor pregnant girls. To make them suffer for their "sin," the nuns compelled them to work in laundries for fourteen hours a day. Then when it was time to give birth, the mothers were denied medication that could ease the pain.

Until only about ten years earlier, the nuns had meted out the ultimate punishment: many babies and their mothers were *killed* and buried on the grounds. But by the fifties, the Catholic church and the Irish government became somewhat more enlightened; the babies were no longer murdered. Their mothers would continue to work in the laundry in the hope that they could earn enough to take their babies away from there.

That never happened because the church and the government did not cease being cruel. They colluded to sell the children of these "evil" mothers to wealthy people in the United States and in Europe.

I was one of those children. Born in 1954, I spent almost the first two years of my life in St. Patrick's Mother and Baby Home in Dublin, where, for the first two weeks, my mother could see me for only fifteen minutes a day—then not at all. She was sent away and forced to leave me behind. I was *stolen* from her.

Almost two years later, the nuns sent me to America, where a couple from Ohio bought me. It may seem that I was one of the lucky ones because I got out alive, but my adoptive mother tortured me from the moment I arrived until the moment I escaped at age sixteen. And though she always told me that my birth mother was dead, I didn't believe it. I never lost hope that I would meet her again one day.

This is the story of my life and my daughter Megan's and my quest to find my birth mother. It's also about the many angels (both earthly and surely not) who first helped me survive my childhood and then supported Megan's and my Irish journey every step of the way.

What Inspired Us to Write This Story

We felt this story had to be told for three important reasons:

- We learned I'm far from the only one: we saw similar stories on our Facebook page (and in the movie *Philomena*). And we've been moved by the stories of so many birth mothers and children who want so much to reunite with their relatives.

- We also want to shed light on the horrors of child

abuse and alcoholism: at the end of this book, we've provided resources for you or any family member or friend who needs protection from them.

- The shameful period is in the news again: as we considered whether to write the book, horrible stories began reemerging in the Irish news as more graves of single mothers' babies are still being discovered at the sites of mother and baby homes.

A Note about Truth

Our story brings you the truth as we know it, or in a few cases, as one of us heard it. In those cases, we relied on the memories of people who are now deceased. All the rest comes from our firsthand experiences. And, I hope you'll agree, what experiences they *are*.

PART I

SURVIVING BY GROWING UP TOO SOON

It's hard to imagine a harder childhood than I was thrown into when I arrived in the US. Ultimately overcoming it would take strength I didn't know I had, and the kindness of friends and strangers.

CHAPTER 1

MY "HOME" IN AMERICA,

PART 1

From the ages of almost two to sixteen (1956–1970), I lived an absolute nightmare. I don't remember ever *not* being cold or afraid in my new home. My adoptive alcoholic mother, Mary, abused me physically, verbally, and emotionally. I quickly learned two things for sure: she hated me, and everything I did made her angry.

Every day until I got old enough to go to school was the same. As soon as she woke, she would start drinking and *keep* drinking and get more enraged as the day went on.

When I wasn't being beaten with her weapon of choice for that day—often a broomstick—I was locked up in a closet or the bathroom for hours at a time. You might find it hard to believe, but I was happier when I was confined, especially in the bathroom. There I could find some comfort and relieve my shivering by sitting against the heating vent.

I spent so much time in that tiny room in a small bungalow in Euclid, a suburb of Cleveland, Ohio, that I'll never forget what it looked like: the tile-covered walls and floors were a maroon brown with pinkish trim. Straight ahead was a window, through which, when I learned how to open it, the kind neighbor lady would hand me treats. The houses were too close together and Mary was too loud for the brick walls to contain her rage. But in those days, people didn't tend to interfere with domestic abuse.

The biggest advantage of being locked away was that Mary couldn't beat me then—*or* when she passed out after downing her daily fifth of Irish whiskey.

After a while, I didn't wait for the unintended gift of being locked up. I became good at ducking, darting, and hiding away in a crawl space beneath the basement stairs where she couldn't get at me. She would get as close as she could, though. I can still see her screaming and swearing at me through blood-red-lipstick-stained teeth on her terrifying face—a sight that gave me nightmares. (To this day, I hate seeing anyone wearing red lipstick!) I would just sit there, repeating in my child's mind, "I hate you. I hate you. I hate you."

By the time I was four, the rest of my waking hours were filled with constant demands to clean the house and do the laundry. She worked me to exhaustion—washing and waxing already clean floors, scrubbing the bathroom, pulling weeds, cleaning out the garage *every weekend,* and anything else she could think of to punish me for seemingly ruining her life.

The only time I left the locked basement during the weekends was on Sunday when Mary dressed me up to go to church. There she would soak up praise for having *selflessly* taken in a poor orphan. It was the only time I ever saw her smile. She fooled a lot of people.

My adoptive father, Joe, did not abuse me, but he also didn't protect me. Another victim of Mary's wrath, he stayed away as much as he could, taking on extra hours at work or drinking at the local bar. That was too bad because when he did come home, she screeched at him instead of at me.

One of her frequent rants at Joe was, "It's because of you that I have to go through the agony of this child. You brought her here!" So it does make me wonder what it was that made her agree to adopt.

A quiet man, Joe never responded to her verbal onslaught. (He might not have even heard it. You might say he was blessed, under the circumstances, with hearing loss from a too-close exploding hand grenade on a World War II battlefield.) It was harder for him to ignore her physical violence: she would punch, kick, and push him, pound on his chest, and throw things at him, but he never fought back.

So during his brief periods at home, Joe would retreat to the basement, drink, and fall asleep on the long, cushioned lawn chair he often used as a bed. I never saw him on the weekends; he worked double shifts as a pressman for the *Cleveland Plain Dealer* newspaper. (I don't know where he slept then—maybe at his sister's house.)

Another Adoption

The year after I arrived, Mary and Joe adopted a second unfortunate child from St. Patrick's. When the social worker who brought Michael Joseph Kelly to the house told me, "This is your new brother," I immediately thought, "Oh, no!"

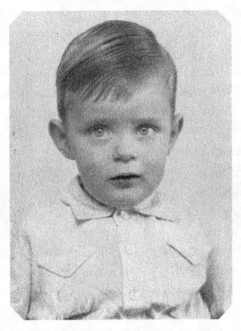

Brother Michael joins the dysfunctional family.

I must have sensed that things would get even worse, and they did. His presence triggered even more hatred and torment. Four-year-old Michael hadn't been there for two hours before Mary shoved him down the basement stairs. A few hours later, his refusal to eat much of her cooking infuriated her enough to shove his face in his food. We had to sit there for hours until he choked down every bite.

I became adept at palming forkfuls to flush down the toilet after that day's release from table captivity, but Michael would just sit there. Later I learned that he had come to us with a problem with his jaw that made chewing painful, which a caring parent—if he'd only had one—would have found out and resolved as quickly as possible.

I also later learned that Mary and Joe chose him, as they chose me, from photos of St. Patrick's "orphans," as if they were buying shoes from a catalog. But Michael was only their second choice of their second adoptive child, their first one having died in the orphanage. It might be easy to blame that disappointment on Mary's mistreatment of Michael—or my undiagnosed attention deficit disorder on her mistreatment of me—but there's no indication that she was ever anything but mean.

For me, misery didn't love company. Michael's arrival generated conflicting feelings: I resented and blamed him because he made my living conditions even worse. It took me a long while to realize that none of it was his fault. At the same time, I felt guilty for not protecting him enough.

Michael and me—the faces of childhood suffering.

And Michael needed protection: it was not until many years later that he would try to help himself—duck or grab the broomstick—let alone fight back. I can't say I would fight back either in those early days, but I did fend off the blows and try to share my evasion tactics with him. But being a sweet, gentle, and withdrawn soul, he suffered much more than I did.

Upon arrival, Michael joined the household routine of being regularly beaten and constantly forced to clean the house. Watching television or playing were out of the question. One day when he was eleven (thinking Mary was passed out), he dared to run out to play ball with some neighborhood boys—but only that once. Mary came raging outside and dragged him by the hair back into the house, a humiliation in front of his schoolmates that seemed to hurt him far more than the physical pain.

Maybe we became *used* to physical pain. Our arms were always scratched, bruised, and sore, and we were always tired—both from cleaning and from Mary's nightly rampages. She would typically wake up at 3 a.m., barge into my room, pull out the drawers, and throw everything out of my closet—all while screaming, "You're a fat pig to leave your room like this! No wonder your mother got rid of you. You're *disgusting!*" Then she would start on Michael and his room.

As exhausted as we were, every evening we were forced to kneel in the living room to say the rosary. If one of us committed the unpardonable sin of slouching, Mary would pull our hair, beat us with the broomstick, and force us to remain there on our knees until dark.

Who *was* this God we were praying to? I couldn't help but wonder why He would take me from my mother and trap me in this awful place. As far as I was concerned for a very long time, He and I were *not* on good terms. I was never suicidal, but there were times that I was so tired, hurt, and miserable that I didn't expect to survive—and I wouldn't much mind if I didn't.

I do recall one time that Joe protected us: when Mary started to wield her weapon, he caught it, retargeting her rage against him. But that was an isolated incident because even when he was around, he wasn't in the habit of standing up to her.

Joe did try to compensate for his absence and Mary's abuse in whatever way he could. In passive response to her tendency to push children down the basement stairs, he unceremoniously built a banister for us to grab onto. And he once put up a Christmas tree and got us both presents, but of course Mary destroyed it all because we "didn't deserve Christmas!" Nor were birthdays ever celebrated.

One day Joe surprised Michael and me with a puppy, which both thrilled and scared us. This would be one more living thing for Mary to mistreat. Within two days, she had kicked the puppy down the basement stairs. We knew exactly how he felt, and we tried to console him. By the next day, the puppy was gone; Joe had rescued him. That's when we gave him a name: Lucky—because he got away.

A Pattern of Neglect

It's a good thing that Michael and I were generally healthy and resilient because if we had needed to depend on Mary to arrange for our medical and dental visits, we would have been in big trouble. Having been adopted through Catholic Charities, we received exams through that organization and Case Western Dental School. They also filled—with *gold*—the mouthful of cavities I'd brought from Ireland. (Yes, it was some of our immigrant *mouths* that were paved with gold, not the fabled streets!)

Catholic Charities occasionally sent a social worker to check on us. Years later, I saw her typed note about me based on multiple visits. It included the line, "The child was sweaty, nervous, and withdrawn." There's no telling for sure why she didn't follow up, but maybe a social worker's ability to act was also limited by the norms of the era.

We quickly became accustomed to being neglected, not only

abused. When I was seven, I took a bath in what I thought was bubble bath because it smelled good. It turned out to be Drano. Days later, Michael and I were hanging laundry out to dry in the backyard when I became feverish and passed out.

Even if Mary had been sober, it's unlikely she would have cared enough to call for help. I might have died if not for the neighbor who found me and sounded the alarm.

I woke up at University Hospital where I stayed for weeks until the doctors figured out why I couldn't move my legs and my kidneys were shutting down. They eventually got me back in "working" order—able to return to work again for Mary. But not before she came to the hospital to castigate me for making her look bad!

Mary and Joe, Before Adopting Children

Here's what I know about the lives of Mary and Joseph (Joe) Hayes in the years leading up to their arrival in my life.

Joe was born in Cleveland, the youngest of seven children in his family struggling through the Great Depression. His grandparents were from County Limerick in Ireland. A quiet and sweet man who loved children, Joe was the godfather to all his siblings' children. His friends described him as a happy drunk who would not hurt a fly.

Mary grew up on a farm in County Mayo, Ireland. I learned from one of her nieces that she was also the victim of cruel nuns at the Catholic school in her small village. As one example of their cruelty, they would tie her favored left hand behind her back to force her to write with her right hand. My best guess of why she was so mean to Michael and me was that her own mistreatment aroused anger that she was not allowed to express in those days. (But, as you'll see, I responded differently.)

She moved to the US when she was in her late thirties, part of a vast emigration of young women seeking employment. In Cleveland, her harsh and fiery demeanor cost her every house-keeping assignment she found.

I can't tell you how she met Joe, only that their tumultuous courtship epitomized the phrase "opposites attract." According to Joe's sister Nancy, it was *his* drinking that caused the tumult; they fought all the time, and then he would disappear for days after a long bender. They eventually married after he vowed to stop drinking. (He didn't stop, though, at least not for decades.)

Because Joe loved children, he talked Mary into trying for one. But they found out that she was unable to conceive a child and that their ages (they wed in their mid-forties) prevented them from adopting a child in the US. That's when they applied to adopt from Ireland through Catholic Charities. They somehow passed "inspection," which amounted only to being Roman Catholic and having "a boatload of money" (said Joe, years later) to pay the adoption fees.

Our Irish "Vacation"

I might have been seven when Mary and Joe took Michael and me to visit her family in County Mayo for a week. The first event that ruined the trip was the disappearance of the chocolate Joe bought to give his brother-in-law Tommy's five children. Mary spent the whole week accusing Michael and me of eating it. I can't speak for him, but I know it wasn't me! I suspected one of Tommy's kids. Or maybe it was Joe, who always had a sweet tooth.

Mary treated us like criminals during that visit, although with uncharacteristic reserve. She hid her true colors, limiting her punishment to discreet squeezes of our arms that were so hard, I thought that mine would fall off. Still, Tommy's wife, whose obviously happy and loved children we envied, saw enough that she tried—unsuccessfully—to lighten the atmosphere: "Oh, Mary, children are children, you know."

Arm squeezes weren't even the worst part of the trip. Whenever we went anywhere in their tiny car, we were packed in so tightly that I had to sit sideways on someone's lap with my feet pushed up against the door. During one outing, I didn't scoot one foot in far enough, and Joe accidentally closed the door on it, breaking four of my toes. I was in pain for days afterward, and he felt awful about it.

There wasn't much for us to do on the farm. As the family went about their daily chores, Michael and I followed them around and tried to stay as far away from Mary as we could.

The only bright spot on that trip should have been the view, but I was in too much pain to appreciate it until I returned years later: a path led from their front door down a hill to a bay and the ocean—the most beautiful place I've seen. Ireland, in general, is gorgeous; it was cruel enough that the nuns robbed me of my mother. They also robbed me of my heritage and the opportunity to grow up in the country of my birth. It's no coincidence that I've always felt bonded with it.

Mary's Influence

The constant fear, chill, and total absence of kind words and comfort in our house certainly took a toll on Michael and me and affected our lives at school. Almost as soon as we walked through the school's doors, it was clear that we were different from other children and their families. Our lack of parental love and care showed: we always looked disheveled, and we were ignored by the others. Fortunately, it was a Catholic school, so we received uniforms, or no doubt our hand-me-down clothes—from our Aunt Nancy's children—would have further set us apart.

But being ignored seemed to suit us so well that we worked hard to avoid notice. We felt embarrassed by our horrible home life, as if it were our fault. As a result, we would never talk about it, and we would never ask for help.

Given all of our cleaning duties, Michael and I could never do our school homework at home. We would scribble it out in the schoolyard before class. I'm grateful that there wasn't nearly as much homework then as children are assigned today. We did just enough to keep the principal from ever summoning Mary for a conference.

Our nutrition was as flawed as our self-images because Mary's cooking was as vile as her temper. The worst dinner of the week was always on Friday and always the same: tuna casserole made with peas and powdered mashed potatoes, which we managed to pretend to eat (Michael caught on eventually). We survived by sneaking Cheez-Its and other edibles that Mary hoarded in cupboards all through the basement. She would never buy one box of anything when she could buy twenty.

Chicken noodle soup was our go-to comfort food. Almost every day after Mary passed out, Michael and I would open and heat up a can.

When we were eight and nine years old, we got an after-school job delivering eggs for a farmer. Our tips from our customers enabled us to supplement our unbalanced diets with drugstore sandwiches and candy. To this day, I haven't lost my craving for Baby Ruth bars.

Joe was no fonder of Mary's cooking than we were, which is one reason—you can guess the other—that he headed to Frank's Bar many nights after work. And pretty much every time, he would order a roast beef sandwich to go with his beer and chasers. Every few weeks starting around the time I was seven, Joe would grant Michael and me the joy of taking us along and buying us each an orange pop and our own roast beef sandwich with real mashed potatoes—two more tastes that remain with me.

Growing up around two alcoholics, I suppose I could have either followed their lead or headed in the opposite direction. I've never been much of a drinker. Michael drank moderately for a time before giving it up; his stomach couldn't tolerate it.

In my mind, I can still hear the revolting sound of a whiskey bottle being opened. That's when I knew the drinking had begun for the day. She started in the morning and was usually crocked by mid-afternoon. By nine o'clock at night, she'd pass out.

Mary was any child's nightmare, and as you can imagine, her daily and nightly terrorizing destroyed Michael's and my self-images for many years afterward. Her most enduringly punishing legacy was verbal. Repeatedly being called disgusting, garbage, a throwaway, a fat pig, and a whore has caused me to feel insecure throughout my life. Those labels became how I saw myself. Later, when I began my first job, I worried that everyone around me saw me the same way.

Mary was particularly obsessed with my weight. I learned on the St. Patrick's Facebook page that the Irish mother-and-baby-home nuns fed the babies solid food at least three months too early so we would look chubby and attractive to prospective adopters. It must have worked on Mary because, as I mentioned, she and Joe chose me from a photograph. But with my stress-eating of junk food to compensate for Mary's cooking, my chubbiness soon turned to overweight, which only attracted more of her contempt—as well as that of my classmates.

I also have Mary to thank for yet another long-term effect of her abuse: all those hours of being confined in tiny spaces made me claustrophobic. I've had to leave places that are too small or crowded. Once on a trip to England, I couldn't make myself walk into Westminster Abbey because of the throngs there.

I saw no escape from the misery Michael and I had been plunged into. But there would be a series of deliverances, both great and small.

CHAPTER 2

MY "HOME" IN AMERICA,

PART 2

My life dramatically changed after my first day in kindergarten when Mary walked me to school. (That's not the motherly gesture it might seem; the school required an escort on the first day.) Later, in front of the whole class, one of my classmates asked me, "Where's your mother? Is that your grandmother?"

"No, that's my mother."

"That *can't* be your mother," he insisted. "She's an old lady."

That got me thinking, so when I got home, I blurted out to Mary, "Where is my mother?" She screamed, "You don't have a mother! She gave you up! She didn't want you because you're worthless and disgusting! Anyway, she died—along with the rest of your family—in a bridge collapse!"

(Starting soon after that tirade and until I was fifteen, my rare periods of sleep were interrupted by the same nightmare: I'm driving halfway onto a bridge over a big body of water when suddenly the guardrails and the car disappear, and water starts pouring over the bridge and sweeping me into it. That's when I would wake up in a cold sweat. And to this day, every time I cross any bridge, even as a passenger, I panic.)

Of course, I was devastated by Mary's rant, but I didn't have to wait too long to find out that she lied. That night, I overheard her muttering to herself, "That little bitch thought she was going to find you, but I made sure she won't. I told her that you and your family are dead."

They say, "The truth will set you free," and it certainly worked for me. For the first time ever, Mary's words, spoken as if to my birth mother, filled me with joy and gratitude. The thought that my mother was actually out there somewhere gave me strength to survive Mary's abuse. Her behavior bothered me less because I could cling to the dream that my birth mother, whom I now yearned for, would rescue me one day. From that moment on, I resolved to be the best person I could and to live my life in a way that would make my mother proud.

Living Angels

What also gave me strength, motivation, and hope was the appearance of angels around me. The first one was Mrs. Steen, that neighbor lady who clearly pitied Michael and me. One Thursday evening, when I was locked in the bathroom, I saw headlights in the driveway of the house next door. I figured out how to crack the window, and Mrs. Steen approached to talk softly with me.

From then on, every Thursday, her bowling night, she would approach to say kind things like, "Don't be afraid" and "Stay strong," while handing me cookies and candy. It helped.

The angel who would turn around my life appeared when I was in the second grade. On my way to school one day, my classmate Kathy Miller waited for me and asked if I wanted to walk with her. That was a big deal because the other kids ignored me, the socially awkward kid. My internal reaction to Kathy's invitation was excitement—I thought, "Wow, she doesn't think I'm disgusting!"

After that day, Kathy and I always walked to school together. One morning, I went back home with her so she could grab a book she'd left behind—an even more pivotal moment because it's when I met her mother. I was waiting on the front step for Kathy, who must have told her mom I was there because soon the door swung open and that kind lady reached down, wrapped me in a huge hug—my first in America—and swept me into her house. She sat me down and handed me a snack. I felt so comfortable there, and I was amazed to learn that everyone in America didn't live the way Michael and I did.

After that revelation—and the best thing that had ever happened to me by then—I went to that house every day before school. Kathy's mom would give me breakfast as her toddlers climbed up on my lap, but it was really her hugs and smiles that drew me. Mrs. Miller smiled with her *eyes*, not just her mouth. There was so much love in that messy, cinnamon-scented house; she showed me what a loving family felt like. And for the first time, I felt accepted.

You can see one of the best illustrations of the vast difference between Mary and Mrs. Miller in this incident at a school music program. As we children swayed to and sang "Too-Ra-Loo-Ra-Loo-Ral," I accidentally bumped the microphone, and it fell over

MEMORY SPARKS

I needed to call up the kind face of my friend Kathy's mother when I dreamed of my birth mother because I didn't retain a mental picture of her. But some images of my few years at St. Patrick's Mother and Baby Home emerged, including the nuns' attire—white habits with big white headpieces that winged out on both sides—and the harsh expression on the face of one particular nun.

loudly. I immediately caught Mary's gaze and projectile-vomited all over the stage. The only thing that kept me from crying was seeing Mrs. Miller's sweet eyes locking onto mine to communicate that things were going to be alright.

From then on, every time I dreamed about my mother, she would look exactly like Kathy Miller's aproned mom with her smiling eyes, her round rosy cheeks, and her dark-brown shoulder-length hair all in disarray. And she would have her gentle touch.

Another angel—and good-mother model—in my early life was Joe's kind sister, Nancy. About once a month, Joe would take

(I don't need a mental picture of stealing that little boy's food or getting smacked for it because I have something else to remember it by: a permanent dent on my nose.)

Decades later, Facebook photos of toddlers standing in big metal cribs at St. Patrick's triggered my memory of standing in a crib like that. And a published picture of two- and three-year-olds outside with nuns really got my attention. I could swear that I'm the child sitting on the lap of the nun on the right.

Compare it with my passport photo and see if you agree.

Michael and me to her comfortable house nearby. We saw Aunt Nancy and Joe's brother, Larry, only at their houses, never at ours, because—surprise, surprise—Mary had alienated his entire family. We were happy during those visits. Nancy talked to us like humans, the way people talked everywhere except in Mary's house.

During those visits, too, Nancy's television introduced us to the popular culture of the time, as we watched *Lassie*, *The Adventures of Ozzie and Harriet*, and *Leave It to Beaver* (themselves models of functional homes kept by loving mothers), and the games of her beloved Cleveland Indians, of whom I later became a lifelong fan. I also became a lifetime fan of hot chocolate after she gave me my first cup.

Victims No More

Time did nothing to mellow Mary, but with every year, she got weaker from a rheumatic heart. I hate to say it, but I especially benefited from her three-month hospital stay to recover from open-heart surgery. Of course, it was news to us that she even had a heart!

In truth, things had been a bit better for us for the two years before her surgery because that's when she started becoming short of breath, which interfered with her ability to chase Michael and me, even when stairs weren't involved.

But Mary's hospital stay was the closest thing Michael and I had ever come to an extended vacation. The relief of not having her around was enormous, and we made the most of it, even though I added household chores to the cleaning already on my plate. In Mary's absence, Aunt Nancy taught me refined household skills, including ironing, grocery shopping, and preparing basic meat-and-potato meals.

Fortunately, Mary's hospitalization also overlapped with the first time I got my period, or I would have suffered even more embarrassment, maybe even trauma. It was Aunt Nancy who brought me a bag of supplies and explained what to do with them. But she didn't tell me it would happen again every month!

The reason Mary had to stay so long in the hospital was that her heart stopped while a nurse was in the room. The nurse performed CPR, and the chest compression not only broke several ribs but sent a blood clot to the brain that gave Mary seizures for the rest of her life.

When she returned home, her new regimen of cardiac and seizure medications plus accelerated drinking and diminished mobility only made her crueler. Even though she was incapable of being as physically abusive as she had been, she did the "best" she could. She also ramped up the verbal abuse: I was ten years old and still a virtual prisoner in her house the first time Mary called me a whore.

But Michael and I were smarter, bolder, and quicker by then. We were *not* going to be Mary's victims anymore. By the time I was ten, Michael and I had bonded and become co-conspirators, sneaking out of the house more often and not caring about the consequences of being caught. That's when we made a pact: whatever it took, we would get out of that house for good as soon as we could. We didn't know what our options were, but having that goal fueled us and further insulated us against Mary.

Expanding Our Worlds, Escaping House Arrest

In the meantime, Michael and I found as much to do beyond the walls of the house as we could. We graduated from our egg route for the farmer to a higher-paying paper route. I loaded the *Sun Post Herald*, our weekly community paper, into a wagon that I pulled around the neighborhood. Michael delivered the daily *Cleveland Plain Dealer* for two years afterward.

At age eleven, I answered a help-wanted sign in the window of a local dry cleaners who hired me to pleat drapes after school (perfect timing; Mary was passed out by then, so she never knew about it). That was almost thirty years after US child labor laws were passed to prevent such things, but their enactors never contended with the need to escape the likes of Mary! The work was a down payment on my ticket out, and I was grateful for it.

Music became another escape for me. My first experience of it was when Mary, at her most plowed and depressed, blared her Irish records at the highest-possible volume. Nothing made me happier; I got to know every word of every song. It wasn't until later that I realized the source of my affinity for that music. My first two years in Ireland—even in unfortunate conditions—were long enough for me to take that country and its culture into my heart and soul.

By the time I was twelve, music and I became even better acquainted. After school, my kind teacher, Sister Boniface, would play songs from *The Sound of Music* on the classroom piano, while four of us girls would stay to clean up the classroom and sing along. One day as we were about to leave, my teacher told me, "You have a lovely voice."

Wow. I didn't get many compliments, and I didn't trust the few I received, because of Mary's negative programming, so I would brush them aside. But as my teacher kept encouraging me, I began to believe her, and I became more confident. I also loved the comfort that music brought me. That's when I branched out.

Rosary ordeals had not managed to sour me on the church. My rebellion took the form of sneaking out to Sunday folk guitar Masses, where I joined the choir and even got to sing solo a few times. You can be sure that a child is repressed when she rebels by going to *church*! But I had to sneak out to attend those Masses because Mary didn't approve of what she and other older parishioners considered a gathering of hippies.

Meanwhile, Michael expressed his new independence by defiantly going to his buddies' houses instead of Mary's after school.

For the next three years, a woman who lived down the street from us asked me to babysit for her four children a few evenings a week when she and her husband went bowling. Mary allowed it on the condition that I give her my wages. But she never got all of my fifty cents an hour for feeding, bathing, and tucking in the kids because she was always too crocked to keep track of my hours, and I hid my earnings in the attic.

I loved the job—for an even better reason than the escape hatch from Mary: I'd been afraid that I was the soulless person Mary claimed I was, because I felt hateful all the time. But my relationship with the children told me something different. Loving and wanting to protect them made me start to realize that I wasn't a bad person.

The more time I spent with that family, the more that welcome feeling took hold. Of course, they were also angels to me. Without their influence, as well as that of the others I've mentioned, I could have gone down a dark path. They continued to support me in every way.

There's no question that these kind people—along with an awareness of my birth mother and a renewed hope of meeting her someday—helped me survive Mary's reign of terror. They too showed me that life was not always painful and that I was not worthless.

Newly bonding with Michael also provided a source of support, as well as getting out in the community and working at whatever jobs I could get at my age. My world had begun to expand; it would grow even more, and not a moment too soon.

CHAPTER 3

ESCAPE

Michael finally reached his breaking point one day when Mary, screaming her head off, summoned the strength to pound on him. The only thing that was unusual about the incident was that it took place outside, in the driveway. Michael was still a gentle soul, but she had humiliated him one time too many, and he hauled off and punched her in the face.

Joe intervened on Mary's behalf and pulled him away, and that—the feeling once again of having no ally, not even in Joe— was the final straw for Michael. Within two months, at age sixteen, he made good on our pact and moved in with his buddy's big family. He lived with them until he joined the Navy a year later.

I lasted at Mary's house for about eighteen months longer, probably because my silent mantra—"I hate you, I hate you…"— helped me to avoid unleashing my anger on her, even as it also made me feel guilty.

My own last-straw moment came another time that Mary rallied her diminishing physical strength. She was in the basement peeling potatoes (she was big on potatoes) when she heard me come home and yelled for me. I can't tell you for sure what set her off that time, because there was *always* something, but it might be that I had come home too late to do the peeling.

As she commanded me to pick up a stack of folded towels on the basement stairs, I heard a growl coming from behind and felt a sting. Using her paring knife, Mary had literally stabbed me in the back! I sprinted up the stairs and locked myself in my bathroom sanctuary so she couldn't stab me again. In that moment while I watched my blood drip onto the tile floor, I knew she would kill me if she got the chance. I knew I needed to get away for good.

As usual, fate and more angels seemed to intercede. I already had a new job, not that it paid anything. Office work, mostly filing, in a local business took the place of my second half-day of school in my senior year. I'd heard about the work-study program from another kind teacher, Sister Monica Marie, who knew that I hated school. But office work was still too sedentary for one who has never been able to sit still for long.

Getting Out

On a bulletin board in the hallway of the office building, I found a handwritten ad for an apartment. It was on the third floor of a house owned by an elderly woman who, fortunately, didn't pick up on the fact that I was too young to rent anything, let alone an apartment.

For $200 a month (dirt cheap even for those times, given the dicey neighborhood), the place had everything I needed—a bed, table, chair, fridge, bathroom, and a location only five minutes by bike from the office. I grabbed it, started living on my own at age sixteen, and remained there for a year and a half.

Soon I could venture beyond biking distance whenever I wanted. At age eighteen and as part of my growing independence, I bought a new car, thanks to a man at the church who co-signed for it. He and his wife—an Irish family—were big fans of the folk Mass, and they'd often invite choir members over for sandwiches after church. The car was a white Honda Civic—with a manual transmission because it was much cheaper than an automatic, but I had no idea how to drive one. I called one of the guys in the choir, and he taught me as much as he could in the dealer's parking lot.

I never quite got the clutch concept, so it took me only eight months to drive that poor car into the ground. Next, I bought a used automatic Volkswagen that tended to stall. The day it died during a snowstorm, I left it on the side of the road, walked three miles to work, and never went back for it. I had been through too much in my childhood to let minor setbacks stop me. From then on, I took the bus.

Almost every night, I ate dinner at Smith's restaurant. I was such a regular that I soon started helping out in the kitchen, and the sweet manager would send me home with food. Once a week, I went to Royal Castle to sit at the counter, order a hamburger and a root beer in a frosted mug, and play "Hey Jude" on the jukebox.

I was slowly emerging from the shell that Mary had stuffed me into, and I was not unfriendly, but my recurring social awkwardness still made it more comfortable for me to be alone. I loved the ability to go to a restaurant or a movie by myself. For the first time in my life, I could do whatever I wanted. Instead of frightening me, my solitary existence made me feel as though a ton had been lifted off my shoulders. I was *free*.

Of course, life still wasn't easy. With the added responsibility of earning enough for the rent, food, and my car payments, I lived on a shoestring. But again, after Mary, I didn't consider it (or much of anything else!) to be a burden.

Life Starts to Fall into Place

The next series of events, like most of the others we describe in this book, certainly seem to suggest angelic intervention. Although I had fled Mary's house, I had no definite plan. But, one by one, opportunities came my way as if every one of them was meant to be.

When I was still a high-school senior, I saw a huge sign in the school's foyer announcing a Catholic Youth Organization singing contest. I decided to enter it, not because I thought I had a chance to win, but because I just thought it might be fun. But I was so nervous, my hands shook—until Sister Monica Marie advised me to focus on the song instead of on myself.

No one was more surprised than I was when I won first prize. I think the win had something to do with my being the only finalist who accompanied herself on an instrument—a borrowed guitar. I had learned the four chords needed for my song, "Today (While the Blossoms Still Cling to the Vine)," from the same boy who had tried to teach me the stick shift.

My prize, payable after graduation, was a scholarship to a school for cosmetology, for which, everyone involved quickly discovered, I had no aptitude. (Do you think it had anything to do with spilling my cup of lukewarm chicken noodle soup on the hair of a customer? Or maybe it was my inability to stop laughing as more and more noodles kept coming out during the rinse.)

The school's owner put me to work at the cash register at the school's beauty supply shop for the next six months, ending shortly after he put his hand up my skirt and made sexual comments. It frightened me, and I stayed away from him for the rest of the day. After that, I didn't return.

I confided in Brother Corrigan, an acquaintance from the folk Mass, who told me that a teacher at the local nursing school was looking for a live-in nanny. He put in a good word for me, and I moved in within a week.

My First Loving Home

Ellen and Tom, who happened to be Irish, all but adopted me as part of their family. Living there felt like *paradise*. Given such consistent kindness, validation, and support, I started to feel almost human. It was at their home that I enjoyed my first real Christmas.

Because Ellen and Tom worked full time, I got plenty of time to look after their adorable sons, ages two, four, and six. I loved every moment. Having endured Mary's mistreatment and absorbed Mrs. Miller's kindness, I wanted only to protect and love children. (Michael had a different reaction; he avoided them for the rest of his life out of fear that Mary's behavior had rubbed off on him.)

To keep busy when the kids were in school, I got a part-time job at the lunch counter of Higbee's, a Cleveland department store. I spent seven happy months like this when Ellen asked me whether I'd ever thought about being a nurse. Um, no. She said she had watched me with her children and thought I might make a good one. The next day, she brought home an application for a full scholarship to the school where she worked.

Being able to take care of children as a hands-on nurse certainly appealed to me. In fact, it was my dream, even before I knew I could have one.

It was the part about having to go back to school that made me hesitate. I did not want to be embarrassed by my poor performance. Mary had called me "stupid" so often that the feeling could still return to haunt me. But I trusted Ellen, so I filled out the application.

I was accepted, and the thought of working with babies moti-vated me. I thought, "I *have* to do this. I have to figure out *how*."

Almost by accident, I did. Without knowing the proven value of repetition, from day one, I came up with a plan to write down everything I heard in class. At night, I rewrote everything, made flash cards, and studied them over and over on the two buses that took me to school.

My technique worked. For the first time in my life, I felt the joy, pride, and surprise of acing all my tests. And just because I didn't take those aced tests to my previous schools to prove I'm not a loser doesn't mean I didn't think about it!

But I can't minimize my first experience of the power of encour-agement to support learning. It meant *everything*. At night, Ellen would also answer any of my questions about my schoolwork—the opposite of struggling under Mary's roof. A kind word and a kind touch, along with all those uninterrupted sleeps, made all the difference. Ellen had made clear that I didn't have to stay in school if I didn't like it. But as soon as I started getting positive feedback, I not only stayed in school, but I enjoyed it.

I also enjoyed my classmates. I've never been the life of the party, but my social skills improved in nursing school. I would converse and laugh with the other students at lunch. (The day I naively mentioned some friendly ladies I'd met at the bus stop, I was the butt of a good-natured joke. After I described their clothes, one of my colleagues said, "You know they're prostitutes, don't you?" No, I most certainly did not. We all found that hilarious, but I maintained my friendship with the bus ladies, who seemed protective of me.)

And somehow, after the first month and a half of school, my colleagues elected me their class president, a role that mostly consisted of announcing school policy changes. I didn't run for it, so I almost fainted when the instructor called my name. Then I thought it was a joke until the nice girl I'd voted for congratulated me.

If I had known at the outset that the president's duties also included giving the graduation speech at the end of the one-year program, I would have declined the post. Along with my ever-present nervousness, I had no clue what to say about the importance of nursing, and it showed in my first draft.

But a few weeks before graduation, I was assigned to home nursing visits with a man who was in a vegetative state. I showed up every day to find that his wife had already bathed, fed, and dressed him, and she would insist on making me breakfast while she chatted with me. I didn't feel I was doing my job, so after my first day, I consulted my instructor, who assured me that I was doing fine: "His wife needs to take care of him, and she needs your companionship. You're there to provide what the patient or caregiver needs."

I finally had the inspiration to rewrite my speech, titled, "Nursing isn't always straightforward." Of course, I still felt like a nervous wreck for the full ten minutes I spoke in front of about 150 people. But focusing on the message and picturing my birth mother in the audience got me through it.

At the end, I took a deep breath and thought, "Mom, I hope I made you proud." She was always in my mind. I clung to the hope that one day we would find each other, even though I had no idea how, or the resources to make it happen.

My presentation was a hit, and it felt good. I drew applause from the audience, kudos from Ellen and Tom, and a request from the nursing director for a copy of the speech. And on top of providing a loving home and the training for my dream job, Ellen and Tom even threw me a graduation party!

MY PREVIOUS RELATIONSHIP
WITH SCHOOL

I'd hated elementary, middle, and most of high school. In fact, I did so poorly in high school that I lived in fear that I wouldn't graduate. Some days I couldn't drag my weary self to class until at least an hour after it began. I got called into the principal's office a lot.

Fatigue was not my only problem with school, though: I also couldn't sit still for long. (I still can't.) I would raise my hand to go to the bathroom more often than the teachers would permit because they knew what I was up to. My nervousness translated to inability to pay attention; I sang in my head, stared out of windows, and mentally went somewhere else—anything but listen. So I dreaded the humiliation of being called on.

I did manage to scrape by scholastically, probably by osmosis—just being in the same room where the teachers

My Nursing Career Launches

Two days before school ended, in 1976, I applied to two hospitals, including Cleveland Clinic, which offered me my first nursing job, along with another major boost to my morale. It was a teaching hospital, which meant that I would be learning as peers of the residents and interns.

Of course, my confidence had begun growing since I moved in with Ellen, Tom, and their boys, and through daily interactions with people at nursing school. Given the damage done by Mary's name-calling campaigns, I saw a miracle in the fact that I now received positive reactions.

presented the subject matter. And maybe the teachers took pity on me because they knew I came from a troubled home. I passed just enough tests to graduate, but just barely; it really could have gone either way.

Then there were the social aspects. Kathy Miller's family had moved away when we were in the sixth grade. Remaining withdrawn, I didn't make another friend until I was in high school. There I befriended two girls who, like me, were shy and didn't fit into any of the cool cliques.

And I benefited from the special attention of those few angelic teachers: Sister Boniface, who encouraged my singing, and Sister Monica Marie, who did more than tell me about the work-study program. When I, with no mother or sewing machine at home to help, needed to make a dress for a senior home economics project, she whipped it up for me.

But that doesn't mean I had reached an unshakable level of self-esteem. The first time I was told to check on a patient during nursing school, I panicked, hyperventilating outside his room, terrified that he wouldn't like me. The nurse that nudged me into the room assured me that most patients are more concerned with getting help than poorly judging the people who kindly provide it.

More than anything, I wanted to work in pediatrics, which I mentioned in my job interview. There just so happened to be an opening for an LPN in that unit, and it seemed as though I would get it. So my heart sank when I learned that I'd been assigned to a different unit. But I quickly recovered; I figured that I'd gone through a lot worse things in my life, and I would just have to go where I was sent.

Well, where I was sent was another miracle: at the end of general orientation, the nurses dropped us new hires off at our units, working our way up from the bottom floors. I was among the last three, and we were walking into pediatrics. I thought it was for one of the other two nurses because my written assignment placed me in the surgical unit.

The nurse manager said, "We just had another position open up; if you're willing to work the 3 to 11 p.m. shift, it's yours." I was overjoyed. The job could not have fit me better because it gave me the joy of working with children.

Every day, I would finish my nursing chores in time to spend the last two hours with a baby in my arms. Many of these sweet little souls were desperately ill, and I would be angry at God for causing them such suffering.

(In the years since, I've stopped blaming God for anything, including allowing me to be wrested from my mother into Mary's cruel hands. I exchanged the blame for simply coping with whatever came my way—not that it would ever have been simple or maybe even possible if I had not received so much help from kindhearted people.)

I also loved the job because we nurses were included in everything right away; I felt like part of the team. I would stay in that unit for three years, then accept an invitation to work in the office of a group of pediatric doctors.

My First Real Vacation

I was still living rent-free with Ellen and Tom, and after my first year at the hospital, I'd saved up enough time and money to take a vacation. There was no place I wanted to go more than Ireland. I hadn't ever planned a trip before, so once again, Ellen and Tom stepped in to help.

I spent all five days just taking in Dublin. By day, I would walk for hours on end while entertaining the fantasy of running into my mom. I didn't know her name, only that I'd been born at St. Patrick's Mother and Baby Home on Navan Road in Dublin (a detail on an inoculation card I'd found in a trunk at Mary's house). Although it was still in operation by then, I never thought of going there.

But even if I didn't miraculously meet my mother, I figured I was probably treading the same ground that she had once walked on. I felt close to her—as if I'd solidified the connection between us. As if I'd come home.

In the evenings, I couldn't get enough of the music in the pubs. By the end of the trip, I felt that I had breathed Ireland into my soul.

(I can't say that I loved my first adult taste of Irish food, though; in fact, it was terrible. But maybe it was the year—long before tourism had reached Ireland in a big way—or the places I went. In later trips, my opinion changed along with the quality of the food.)

Courting a Loner

Back home at the hospital, I made friends with a wonderful twelve-year-old boy who came in for leukemia treatments. Even when I wasn't working with him, I would visit him a few times a week. One day, I dropped by when he had two other visitors: his mother and a man in his mid twenties.

The next evening, his mother called to ask if I'd noticed the young man. "That's my son's basketball coach," she said. "Jack is a good guy, and he'd like to ask you out." At age twenty-three, I'd never had a date, and having grown up in a repressed environment and having encountered a sexual predator at the beauty school, I didn't want one. I told her that the offer made me uncomfortable. She said, "Why don't you think about it? I'll call you back tomorrow."

My colleagues started working on me, and when my patient's mother called back with a gentle pitch of her own, I reluctantly agreed. Of course, I was nervous through most of the date, a long time to be nervous. With dinner, a movie, and a ride to the airport to watch planes, the date lasted five hours. Through it all, Jack was a gentleman—or I probably would have slapped him!

The next day, he sent roses and called to ask if I'd go out with him again. He also asked if I had any dresses that don't make me look like a nun. I felt embarrassed because I actually did not. Without a flirtatious bone in my body or any interest in clothes, I'd worn a black dress with a high neck and long sleeves on our first date. Besides that and my uniforms, the only clothes I owned were a few shirts and pairs of jeans.

Jack remained attentive anyway, sending me handwritten cards and continuing to take me out. Two weeks after our first date, I later learned, he bought an engagement ring, which he began trying to give me over the next few months. But I had no experience with this kind of relationship, and my insecurity came back to haunt me. I just couldn't see what he saw in me. I turned him down five times.

He didn't give up, and the sixth time was the charm. We were married on September 21, 1979, one year to the day after our first date.

A Living, Breathing Miracle

Two years after the wedding, I got pregnant, which both thrilled and terrified me: I'd worked with women who'd miscarried, so I couldn't help but worry. But I also never felt more alive than when I was pregnant; from the start, I felt like a mother.

The pregnancy and delivery went blessedly well, and the moment my Kate was placed in my arms, I knew that I was holding a gift from God. I committed to letting her know that I loved her and that I would do anything to protect her. I committed to being everything to her that Mary was not to me.

I also made that silent pledge on Kate's behalf to my own mother. This time I wanted to make her proud of the mother I intended to become. Although I didn't know what she went through at my birth, I thought, "If anybody were to take this baby from me, I would kill them!" It pained me that she had experienced pregnancy and childbirth without being able to keep and raise me, for some reason I would not know for a while to come.

Once again, and maybe more vividly than ever, I felt sadness through every cell of my being that my mother was not there with me to share this life-affirming event.

Being away from precious Kate during my first day shift after maternity leave tore my heart in half. I sobbed for most of every day for the first week, until a doctor at work suggested that I switch to nights. Miraculously, a night position opened up in pediatrics at our local hospital, so I started the following week. I was exhausted all the time, but life with Mary had trained me to get by on little sleep and the joy of days with my baby was worth exhaustion.

After about nine months of this routine, a nurse recommended the day care center in the hospital. I looked at it, but the place reminded me too much of an orphanage to trust my Kate to it. I would stay on the night shift for thirty years, napping when I could. When Kate, and my children to come, Tim and Megan, were in grade school, I could be home in time to take them to school and take in every one of their events. Although I was always tired, I was as happy as a lark.

Tim, Megan, and Kate

Deliverance from Evil

Michael and I had fled Mary's violence because we were guided along our own paths towards acceptance and empowerment. Michael found his home in the Navy, where he stayed for twenty-two years.

For me, inspired by Ellen and Tom's positive feedback, my personality began to blossom. Everything that happened empowered me, from leaving Mary's house at age sixteen and a half to living solo through my tenure as a nanny.

After I'd been with Ellen's family for a year, I had grown into a different person than the nervous refugee from Mary's house. I no longer felt like an ugly duckling without value. I was living in a loving home where I basked in the feelings of security, comfort, and support. And the family trusted me to take care of three little boys I adored. Despite, or maybe because of, my upbringing, being kind to children felt like the most natural thing in the world.

Making my way through nursing school and into my career brought me even more confidence. Most of my remaining insecurity vanished the moment I held my baby. I felt *powerful*. I would let no one stop me from treasuring my child. From that moment on, I would devote my life to my child and my children to come.

I also had what you might call a kind of religious experience. As a child at Mary's house, I had rejected the idea of God's love; I'd blamed Him for my circumstances and was sure He didn't think much of me. But now, holding Kate, I got the overwhelming feeling that He must actually love me to send me this beautiful gift. (That feeling was reinforced twice more, when I gave birth next to Tim and then to Megan.)

If everything hadn't happened exactly as it did, I doubt that I would have made it to nursing school and fulfilled my purpose as a pediatric nurse. And without nursing, it's also doubtful that I would have met the persistent man with whom I would fulfill my dream of being a mother and then a grandmother. But I'm getting a bit ahead of myself.

CHAPTER 4

MY LATER RELATIONSHIPS WITH MARY, JOE, AND MICHAEL

As far as I know, Mary never went looking for me after I escaped, and she had the means. She got her first driver's license when she turned fifty-five, but she didn't have it for long. Joe told me that while she was driving drunk, she caused a six-car pileup including injuries and an insurance nightmare.

My absence caused her to ramp up terrorizing Joe, but it also had a positive effect on him. While Michael and I still lived in the house, he had tried and failed five times to get sober. Michael and I would have to hold him down on the bed while he suffered from delirium tremens of withdrawal during those unsuccessful attempts. But nothing stuck until I moved out, which he said made him realize how much he had wronged Michael and me. He also credited the encouragement of his sponsor at the addiction program he joined.

As part of Joe's successful path to sobriety, he wanted to ask me for forgiveness. One day, his sister Nancy called me to say, "Your father has had a breakthrough with his alcoholism, and he would like to talk with you. Would you meet him at my house?"

Good question. I was leery about what was going to happen. On the other hand, I also didn't want to feel guilty for not going. So I went but without letting my guard down, even physically. While Joe sat on the living room sofa, I stood by the banister, ready to run at any moment.

Whether drunk or sober, Joe had always been quiet. This day was the first and only time I ever heard him speak a full paragraph. That must be why I recall almost every word: "I just want to tell you I'm really, really sorry that I didn't protect you from what happened to you. I didn't have it in me to help you because I couldn't get out from under my drinking and Mary's control. I dropped the ball, and I hope it isn't too late to make amends."

He wasn't just checking a twelve-step box. He was clearly distraught; tears ran down the face of this man who never had before shown me emotion. He was tormented by guilt that our trips to Nancy's house or to Frank's Bar, a banister, and a temporary gift of a puppy were all he was able to do for us. They were far from what we needed most from him, and he knew it.

The more he talked, the more I empathized, so I granted his request for forgiveness. It didn't cost me much, and it seemed to take a weight from his shoulders. And although I had been angry at him for all but deserting Michael and me, I had never despised him. For a long time, I'd felt that he was just one more of Mary's victims.

I was happy that he had finally let go of the grip of his terrible addiction to drinking. However, I can't say that forgiving him meant forgetting or that I was ready to hop into a rebuilt relationship with him. I proceeded in delicate baby steps. I brought my fiancé to meet him and Mary, and they both attended our wedding. My husband, Jack, and I visited their house every month. After she was bedridden we would take him every Sunday to a restaurant Joe liked. Every one of those visits were for him, never for her.

Sorry, Not Sorry

I never did and never will forgive Mary, and Joe knew better than to ask me to. But he did ask me to help her. Physically, she was failing. By the time Kate was born, Mary was bedridden and in need of home care, which meant she couldn't get to her whiskey or go on tirades. "Would you come to bathe her?" he asked me.

Because I'm a nurse, I agreed to do my job, but not as a daughter and totally without a shred of tenderness. I did that job quickly and robotically. I didn't speak to her, I hated being in that house, and I didn't stay a minute longer than I had to. Even the sight of that ugly plastic-covered pea-green couch would mentally transport me back to all those hours forced to kneel in front of it and say the rosary.

(The furniture was never changed the whole time they lived there, including two end tables with sharp corners. I can't even count the number of times Joe called Jack and me to help tend to a bleeding Mary who had fallen onto the glass tabletop after she had a seizure.)

Joe stayed with Mary for the rest of her life. It's hard to say if he loved her; I never observed any affection between them.

But he honored the obligation that he felt he had to her. And I believe his guilt about how things turned out included how they turned out for her.

Years before, when I still lived at their house, Joe's guilt toward Michael had inspired a road trip—with me at the wheel, only two days after I got my driver's license. Michael, newly enlisted in the Navy, was in boot camp at a base near Chicago, Illinois. This was before Joe beat drinking. When I returned from school one afternoon, waiting for me in the car was Joe—drunk and feeling sorry for himself because Michael had left. After asking me to drive him to see Michael, he crawled into the back seat and slept through the six-hour drive.

I found my way to Chicago in part from memory—I'd gone along with Joe a few times to collect cases of whiskey that Mary's brother procured on the cheap—and by stopping at gas stations for directions. We visited with Michael for an awkward couple of hours before heading back.

Joe never asked Michael to forgive him, maybe because he knew that Michael never would. As Michael described it, Joe had been "a grown-ass man who chose to ignore that his children were being abused."

So I was surprised when, twelve years after the road trip, Michael agreed to give the *abuser* a fair hearing. Her hospice nurse had told me that Mary wanted to apologize for how horribly she had treated us. I immediately turned down the offer, while he came from Alabama in the hope of letting go of his hatred toward her.

It turned out that Mary couldn't pass up this final opportunity to exert control and wreak terror. When Michael showed up at her bedside, she would not say a word to him, though she was still able to talk. He left devastated, and of course, I felt awful for him.

Joe Survived Mary

It wasn't until sober Joe buried Mary in 1990 that he was free to live peacefully. He spent his days taking candy to the bank tellers in six different branches of the same bank where he kept small balances. In between, he would visit his sister, go to meetings of Alcoholics Anonymous and to church, and sit in the sun in a brown-striped lawn chair in his front yard and feed the squirrels.

He continued to love children, and he loved sports, so he also loved to go to see my younger kids play in their school games. His eyes would light up at the sight of Megan, whom he called his "little chickadee" and to whom he would sing, "I love you, a bushel and a peck…"

When Joe developed Alzheimer's disease in 1997 and could no longer take care of himself, Jack and I brought him and his striped lawn chair to live with us. He also seemed to have developed an inadvertent sense of humor. One day, as we were having lunch on the glass tabletop on our patio, the wind picked up, then dropped the umbrella along with the table it was attached to, smashing the glass. He looked at me and said, "Do we have to pay for that?" I said, "Of course," to which he replied, "Then let's get the hell out of here!"

Joe's Enduring Legacy

I continued to work nights, so it took all five of us to keep an eye on Joe. Alzheimer's disease is a tragic way to live, but caring for him also turned out to be a gift he gave us. Two months after he passed away, in 2002, Jack showed me a newspaper article about adult foster care, which I had never heard of. I immediately thought, "I can do that."

Before that experience with Joe, I wouldn't have thought I

could, especially after I was sent from my hospital's pediatric unit to feed an elderly patient. When I leaned over to say, "Good morning," he rewarded me by spitting in my eye and kicking me in the shin. I was never so happy to return to my unit or more grateful that he had not been my first hospital patient.

So at that point, I thought there was no way in Hades that I would ever take elderly people into my house—until it happened, almost in the blink of an eye. I applied and was approved for a license from the Department of Aging to care for two residents. Jack made a pamphlet advertising our new family business and, just a week later, welcomed our first non-relative, who stayed with us for six years. Then I got a license for five residents.

All the while I was taking care of our residents and my family, I held onto my hospital job. The routine was pretty much the same every day: I'd come home from my twelve-hour night shift, give the residents breakfast and a bath, and take a nap when they did until it was time to give them lunch. Then they'd nap again while I stripped beds, did the laundry, and maybe grabbed another nap before dinner. This went on for twelve years, and believe it or not, I loved it.

Then I "retired" and went to work for Megan's company, where I remain to this day. *She* so enjoyed working with the elderly folks living in our house that even while she was still in college, she decided she would make it her business. She worked as a marketing director at an assisted living facility to fund the residential care home she founded after she graduated. She has owned and operated Heart & Home in Cleveland since 2009.

Megan has also been blessed by the guidance of angels. Each of five times that she has faced a major business or life decision, she has seen a sign (usually literally, like the one at a petting zoo with baby chicks) saying, "Come pet our little chickadees," Joe's nickname for her. Or she would run across a song or ad with the words, "I love you a bushel and a peck." For her, it was a clear message from her grandfather that she's on the right path. And that favored path always ends up working out for her.

Bonding and Grief

In March of 2005, my adoptive brother left me this blunt voice message: "Hey, Marie. Just wanted you to know I probably have only three days to live."

It turned out that it was only one possibility. Michael, who smoked four packs of cigarettes a day, had a tumor on his lung that threatened to press against an artery. The equally blunt doctor at the hospital had told him, "We'll put you on steroids. If they don't work, you could die. But if you survive the weekend, we'll start you on chemotherapy and radiation."

Michael made it, and the next month, I flew to Hoover, Alabama, to be with him. I can still picture coming down the escalator to the baggage claim area and getting my first glance of that tall, sweet guy leaning against a pillar.

We had barely seen each other over the years, but there was no awkwardness between us. Of course, I was shocked to see him so weak and gaunt. He asked, "Do you think you could make me some food? I haven't been eating much." The radiation and the chemotherapy he'd received that week had wiped him out.

He specifically wanted chicken noodle soup and bacon, eggs, and toast. We stocked up at a grocery store on the way to his house, which reeked of smoke from the tobacco that no doubt caused the tumor. I went for so many walks just to breathe fresh air that I lost ten pounds that week.

We had barely stepped inside the door before Michael showed

off his many awards. He earned them as a master chief petty officer on Navy submarines stationed for six months at a time to observe countries like Iran and Iraq. (Unlike me, he was clearly *not* claustrophobic.) He was justifiably proud of his work, and he had found his tribe there. Best of all, despite all the baggage he carried from childhood, he had found happiness.

We lived a whole lifetime during that week. It felt so natural for me to take care of him, almost as though I were his mother. I cooked for him, took him outside, put him to bed, massaged him, and washed his back because the radiation had affected his bones so much that he could barely lift his arms.

Through it all we talked and talked. We both found it hard to say goodbye at the end of that week, and we stayed in frequent touch by phone. Although his health rallied at various points after that, about ten months later he called to say, "I want you to know that my doctor said there's nothing more he can do for me. He's stopping all treatment."

The news devastated me. We had grown so close during our week together, and I wanted more time with him. We would not have the chance. His friend called two days later—on St. Patrick's Day, one year to the day from his diagnosis—to say that my brother, Michael Kelly, had passed at 2 a.m. (Only the day before, she said, he had rallied, putting on Irish music and trying to dance a jig.)

Still, I was glad that he didn't have to suffer anymore. When I returned to Alabama to plan the funeral, I learned more about Michael from his tightly knit circle of friends. They said he was so kind that he would give you the shirt off his back and then go out to buy you a new one. That circle included the minister who gave the eulogy, saying that although the start of Michael's life had been dark, the man they had known was full of light and goodness.

Then the minister turned to me. "Marie, I want you to know this. Michael said that the happiest thing that ever happened to him was becoming friends with you." As you can probably imagine, his words devastated me.

I was still reeling from the gut punch of losing Michael when my dearest friend, Connie, called to break the awful news that she had been diagnosed with untreatable kidney cancer. She died in late January of the following year. Her kids were getting married; it broke my heart to know Connie would never get to cuddle their babies, and, of course, that I would never see her again.

One of her daughters said that her mother had two last requests: to be buried in her favorite T-shirt, jeans, and tennis shoes; and for me to sing at her Mass. "Oh no, honey," I said, "I'm not going to be able to do that." Feelings of guilt took over by the next day: how could I *not* do the last thing my best friend would ever ask of me? I called back and said yes, even as I was fighting a respiratory infection.

I was hoarse when I walked into the church, early so I could practice with the organist. By luck or by angels, it happened to be the third day of February, when Catholics celebrate the sacrament of the Blessing of the Throats. I got in line and received it. And wouldn't you know my voice was perfectly clear when the Mass started!

I imagined Connie working it out with God, saying, "Look, my whole family will be there, and I don't want this to go badly. Could You please just lay the healing on a little thicker for Marie?"

My Family Evolution

Although I won't forgive Mary, time and maturity have made me understand that her treatment of Michael, Joe, and me must have been the result of an undiagnosed mental illness, even before factoring in her alcoholism. She was a tortured soul. We're fortunate that she ultimately lost her power over us. We overcame her negative influence and went on to live in peace and freedom with our pasts truly behind us.

I'll always be grateful for the relationship I developed with Joe, starting with his sobriety and apology, and Michael in those later years. It was a special joy to be given that time.

The week I spent with Michael the year before he died also had a positive effect on my physical fitness. I gained a now-permanent walking habit and started favoring salads over desserts. I lost ninety more pounds over the next two years. (Take that, Mary!)

It's not like me to express grief in front of the people I love, so my walks also became emotionally cathartic. I used them to cry and talk to Michael and Connie, while I listened to Brad Paisley's "When I Get Where I'm Going," and Vince Gill's "Go Rest High on That Mountain," two of the songs we played at Michael's funeral.

I would not have known how to draw Joe and Michael into my family if Kathy Miller's mom, and Ellen and Tom, had not shown me what real family looks like. I'll always be in their debt for embracing me.

PART II

THE QUEST

*Now that our children were grown,
I had the time, but not the means,
to look for the mother I'd always
felt in my heart.*

*As Megan learned more of my story,
she became committed to helping me
find her. And once she sets her mind to
something, stand back! Megan turned
up clues and pursued them, endlessly
encouraged me, and planned and
funded our trips to Ireland so we
could follow the trail.*

CHAPTER 5

STARTING THE SEARCH FOR MY BIRTH MOTHER

The desire to find my mother never went away. But as time went on, fulfilling it seemed less and less possible. I no longer believed that she was coming for me. I was all but resigned to meet her only in heaven, *if* I'd been good enough in life to make it there someday, which didn't feel like a shoo-in!

In early 2005, Aunt Nancy's daughter, Pat, shared with Michael and me the contact information of a social worker in Ireland who had knowledge of St. Patrick's Mother and Baby Home. We wrote to her separately without any idea if we'd hear back. So many months passed that I'd almost forgotten that I'd written. Then a letter arrived.

I was shocked and overjoyed to receive it, and then to read its contents: At age fifty-one, for the first time in my life, I learned my birth mother's name: Anastasia O'Leary. The letter also contained my full name at birth and birth date and time: Maria Goretti O'Leary, born November 5, 1954, at 10 p.m. It read, "Your mother stayed with you for two years. She breastfed you…"

(Later, while comparing notes with Michael, I found out he got a letter that was the same in every respect except for his two unique facts: Una Kelly was his mother's name, and he was born on September 30, 1953. His letter did not state the time of birth. I began to question the authenticity of our letters because it turned out that everyone received that form letter, but we learned we could trust what was unique about them. Michael was as happy as I was to receive his letter; he said he knew he had no time to search for his mother, but, in one of the last things he ever said to me, he urged me to keep looking for mine.)

It meant so much to hold even that printed connection to my mother. Just recalling it now gives me goose bumps. I read it over and over, shared it with my husband, and slept with it under my pillow for weeks. I also mentioned it to Eve Hill, my friend at work, who had often urged me to see what I could find out. But I was so busy and tired from working my night shift and caring for elderly people in my home that it would be years before I pursued the clues we had or looked for more.

That changed in 2013, when I received a voicemail from Eve telling me I needed to see a new movie called *Philomena* because, she said, it's my story. It's actually based on the true story of the search by a journalist and an Irish birth mother to find the son taken from her in a mother and baby home. I rushed to see it, and it hit me like a ton of bricks. There I was in the back row, sobbing my eyes out, especially when they took away the mother's baby.

By the time the film ended, I was both angry and empathetic about the pain and suffering my own mother must have gone through, which had rarely crossed my mind. For most of the time before that, when I thought of growing up without her, I'd felt sorry only for myself. I'd imagined that she gave me up because she couldn't afford a child.

Along with my letter, the movie awakened my desire to work on finding my mother. I started by reading as much as I could about Irish mother and baby homes, and by then, there was a lot to read about them. Women who'd been forced into those places were coming out of the woodwork to tell their stories of coercion and horrific abuse. The story had also resurfaced with the discovery of mass graves—the murdered babies of the shamed single mothers.

Eve told me about a private investigator she'd seen on TV who specializes in reuniting families and would conduct a search for a fee. But I didn't have the money for anything like that. Even if I could have afforded it, I wouldn't have known who to trust, especially in a different country, so I put the idea aside.

Fortunately, Megan, who didn't want me to have to wait until the afterlife to meet my mother, took the lead. She'll tell this part:

Fate, Facebook, and I (Megan) Intercede

Marie (as I'll call my mom in this book) had shared her story with me piece by piece as our mother–daughter friendship grew through the years. She had always been such a great mother that, when I was a kid, I told my friends that she must be an actual angel, with wings hidden in there somewhere. So it deeply saddened me to learn that she had been cheated out of a relationship with *her* mom. As soon as I was old enough, I vowed to see what I could do about this.

Of course, it didn't hurt that the search would involve a visit to Ireland. Marie had instilled in my siblings and me a deep love for that glorious country. She would play Irish music in the house, Mary's side of the family would come to visit us from Ireland, and we would celebrate every St. Patrick's Day as if it were a second Christmas. For me, that love crystallized when I was twenty-three, and my boyfriend Connor and I became engaged on a vacation in Ireland.

By the following year, Connor had become my husband, and Marie had been expressing fresh interest in searching for her mother. He and I planned another vacation to Ireland, this time with Marie. We didn't have much to go on, but Eve suggested that we take Marie's Catholic Charities letter to the Dublin records office and search for birth certificates in her mother's name.

Good thing that name wasn't Bridget, Colleen, or some other common Irish one. We found five birth certificates—two of them with accompanying death certificates—for Anastasia O'Learys in the likely age range.

We didn't know what to do with that information, so we mentally filed it away and spent the rest of the week soaking in Ireland. When we got home, I looked up St. Patrick's Mother and Baby Home on Facebook where I learned that people who had tried to get information were told that a fire had destroyed the institution's records. That seemed to happen in these places far too often to be true, and it wasn't.

I also found a Facebook page where former residents (kids and occasionally mothers) would go to seek their lost relatives. It was full of sad stories about mothers who, when found by their children, refused to acknowledge them, let alone meet them. These women had been made to feel so much shame that many of them probably took their secrets to their graves. In some other cases, the children the women had after they married felt threatened by the idea of a new sibling showing up.

Most of the tales I read were negative, and I worried about a tragic ending to our search. But the few happy stories motivated me, and of course I hoped Marie would be among that minority. My father set up a Facebook page for her, where she followed the stories and occasionally posted a request: "Do you know of someone by the name of Anastasia O'Leary? I'm looking for my mother."

For two years, nothing came of that request.

Then, out of the blue, something did.

We owe so much to a series of people who went out of their way to help total strangers. *Why* did they? Well, I've got to tell you, with the exceptions of Mary and everyone who was responsible for the baby market, Irish people are among the most generous and hospitable we've ever known. And given all the stories that have emerged in recent years about the atrocities committed way back when at mother and baby homes, people were especially motivated to help us.

Enter Kind Total Stranger #1

(Marie will pick up the story from here.) The Facebook page opened a whole new world for me. Stunned to see posts from so many other people who were born where I was, I became a frequent visitor to Facebook. One amazing day in 2016, I saw the story and photo of a man who had helped to reunite a family that was separated at St. Patrick's. I wasted no time reaching out to ask him if he could help me, too.

He responded quickly but discouragingly. He couldn't take on my search, he wrote, because he got so invested in the previous one that it exhausted him. Of course, I was disappointed to see that glimmer of hope go out, but I understood his feeling and told him so.

By the next day, Mick McNulty had reconsidered, writing, "It seems that I can't *not* help you. Tell me your story." When I wrote back, this kind soul started us on the path we hadn't been able to find on our own—and he refused any payment. He did this type of work as a labor of love. It began when he helped his wife find her son; the joy it brought her inspired him to help others.

Once this good man signed on to help us, he never gave up. I sent him copies of the few documents I had, and he asked me to write a blog he could post on various websites that reunite families. Mick wisely advised me to write that my adoptive family had treated me well. He said that telling the truth about them might scare away my birth mother and her family. For the same reason, he said to include this sentence: "I bear no ill will towards you."

Suddenly, everything started to feel too real, so when Mick also advised me to take a DNA test, I put it off indefinitely.

Kind Total Stranger #2

I was at work about five months later, now 2017, when I received a Facebook message from Paul Little. He wrote, "I saw your post. I'm a crib mate of yours from St. Patrick's Home, and I believe I know where your mother is. Here's my phone number. Please call me." I was so stunned that I dropped the phone, sat frozen for ten minutes, and read the message again, struggling to process it.

I remained too stunned to respond. I was also late: it happened to be St. Patrick's Day, and I was going to meet my family for our traditional celebration.

(By the way, in the context of a mother and baby home, "crib mate" doesn't necessarily refer to someone who was there during the same timeframe; the term is used to mean someone who passed through the same place. In that way, it's like "alumni," which refers to graduates of the same school in any year.)

When I got to Mavis Winkle's Irish Pub just outside of Cleveland, I showed the message to Megan, who insisted I call Paul right away. Paul picked up on the first ring, and his news knocked me on my butt: he told me that an acquaintance of his takes care of an elderly woman named Anastasia O'Leary near the location where we thought—based on the five birth certificates we found—my mother might have been born!

After all those years of wishing for my birth mother, our prayers appeared to be answered, and she seemed to be within reach. Never for a second did it occur to Megan or me that the lady in question might *not* be my mother.

It seemed to occur to Paul, though, and he offered to do some investigative work. "The caregiver takes Ms. O'Leary to the post office once a week," he said. "I'll be there when they show up, and I'll take her picture so we can see if she looks like yours," referring to the photo of myself I had posted in the blog.

I told Mick about this new development, and once again, he urged me to do a DNA test. After having procrastinated for three months, I set that in motion, then nervously waited the five weeks it took to receive the results.

Kind Total Strangers #3 and #4

In the meantime, Paul's caregiving acquaintance, citing patient privacy, nixed the idea of his investigative work, so I intensified mine. On Facebook in general, not just on the St. Patrick's page, Megan reached out to every single O'Leary living in that area of Ireland, asking, "Do you have a relative named Anastasia?" She shared the story with the few people who wanted to know why she had asked. That's when "Big Noel" came into the picture.

An O'Leary, but no relation, Noel offered to drive the hour and a half to where Anastasia had been spotted! Of course, Megan and I were grateful for his generous offer, but we gently turned it down. Assuming the lady was my mother, we had no idea how—or

whether—she would receive me or even the news that I was looking for her. The social stigma of unwed motherhood had been so deeply embedded that an encounter would be a sensitive situation; we knew we needed to put a lot of thought into how to approach it.

Two days later, Megan got a message from another O'Leary, again no relation, but *a neighbor of Anastasia!* She said, "I'm going to walk over there and ask her about you!" *No!* "Please don't do that," Megan responded. "I don't want to scare her." But with the time difference, she got the message only after the deed was done. She wrote back, "Anastasia said she never had any children at all and never set foot in Dublin during those years. But she told me to ask you to please give her a call."

Well, *that* started our wheels spinning! "Ha!" Megan said. "It must be her! Why else would she want you to call her? She probably just didn't want her neighbor to know!" Megan sat next to me as I, with trembling hands, dialed the number. The woman named Anastasia answered and gently repeated what she'd told her neighbor. We still weren't convinced, especially when she ended the call with, "If you're ever in Ireland on my side of town, please stop by and we'll have a cup of tea."

Megan told me, "Sure. We'll show up, and this Ms. O'Leary will look exactly like you!"

In fact, we were so sure of that outcome that Mick began building a family tree based on her location and known relatives. That tree was superseded within a week when the DNA results came back. As Mick said, "People lie, but DNA doesn't. That's not your mom." Now Mick had accurate information for my family tree.

Then what exactly was behind this Anastasia's invitation? We've since come to learn that it's just one more example of Irish hospitality. Meanwhile, we figured that the poor woman was probably being ostracized in her village, or at least thought to have had a secret baby! To try to make up for any embarrassment we'd caused her, Megan sent flowers.

The Cousins Connection

My DNA linked my mother to a different geographic area than the one inhabited by the Anastasia we spoke to. The connection to two towns—Blessington and Kiltegan—was based on finding second cousins, which amazed him. "That's a strong DNA link," he said. "It means that, beyond a shadow of a doubt, this is where you're from. The best we usually get is fourth and fifth cousins."

Then Mick said, "You need to get your boots on the ground. Fly to Ireland, drive to those towns, and hit up every pub and church there. If anybody knows anybody in a small village in Ireland, that's where you'll find 'em."

Megan sprang into action and started planning our second trip; we would leave for Ireland on August 25, 2017. In the two weeks before our departure, so much kept falling into our laps. Mick supplied more cousins' names, and the family tree began to grow.

Stressed!

The whole experience filled me with such anxiety that I barely slept or ate. I thought, "Oh my God, what are we doing? Megan is going all out to arrange this for me. What if this is the biggest mistake ever? What if it turns up *nothing*?" My anxiety also sent me in a couple of other directions:

A Visit to a Psychic

Seeking answers in the absence of them, I was drawn—three days before departure—by a "Psychic Readings" sign on a large white office building in the nearby city of Parma Heights. I called the phone number on the sign and made an appointment for the same day.

"What am I doing?" I thought as I pulled into the parking lot. I didn't know what to expect. I'd never been to a psychic; I didn't hold much stock in them, to be honest, but you know what they say about desperate times calling for desperate measures? I figured I had nothing to lose but twenty-five dollars, and what if there were something to this? But I was embarrassed enough about embarking on this field trip that I didn't tell anyone, not even Megan.

At the appointed time, I walked through the lobby of a building filled with lawyers' and accountants' offices and rode the elevator to a waiting room that was barely bigger than its modest couch. Another client there struck up a conversation with me. "Is this your first time? The psychic is very helpful," she said. "I think you'll like her."

At that moment, the door to the inner office opened, and there stood Miss Bonnie, a woman in her midsixties who physically resembled Mrs. Doubtfire, the role Robin Williams played in the 1993 movie by the same name. Dressed in an old-fashioned buttoned-up blouse and a long dark skirt, she wore big-frame glasses (a few years before they were in style) and full, curly, chin-length gray hair.

She had come out to scold us. "With all this chatter, I cannot listen to everything I need to!" With that, she closed the door, and the other woman and I just looked at each other. I contemplated leaving but ultimately decided to take a chance.

The skeptic in me had formed a plan: I was not going to volunteer any information. So when it was my turn to enter the tiny inner office and sit across from her desk, I simply said, "I've got some things happening in my life, and I'm wondering if you could give me a feel for them."

She didn't say anything for a bit, then things quickly got weird. At various times, her head would snap up, eyes wide, and she'd start talking over her shoulder to invisible beings, saying things like, "Yes, I *know!* I'll tell her." I was both fascinated and creeped out, thinking, "This woman is a *kook.*"

After a few minutes of what sounded like a monologue, she turned her attention to me. "First of all, I can tell you that you have many angels around you. I'm picking up the name Michael. This Michael is significant to you."

Interesting. My first thought was, "That must be my birth father's name." Then she got that idea out of my mind with, "It's probably the Archangel Michael." She went on to say, "I sense that you've been in darkness, and he has been protecting you. He still is."

What came next knocked my socks off and gave me goose bumps: "You're going on a journey, it's the right time, and the angels will go with you."

With that, she allayed my fears a bit—about the trip and about her. This woman who had struck me as a crackpot might, in fact, be the real deal. Of course, I'd known for years that angels had looked after me, but now I had both confirmation and new information.

After that mind-blowing session, I just went back to work, keeping everything to myself, as if nothing had happened. I tried to focus on the many loose ends I needed to tie up before the trip.

(It was not until 2021, a few weeks after Megan and I started writing this book, that the realization washed over me—while I was stopped at a red light!—just which Michael the psychic had sensed. After my adoptive brother died, *he* sent angels to guide me because it had been his dying wish that I find my mother. It was also one of the last things he said to me in person.)

A Visit to the Adoption Agency

At the Catholic Charities office, right down the road from me in Cleveland, I asked whether they had any documentation of my adoption. Two days before we left, a letter arrived that provided another piece of the puzzle. It stated that I was born at St. Patrick's Mother and Baby Home to a twenty-eight-year-old woman who, when she was in the sixth grade, had quit school to help her mother raise her thirteen siblings. She had been working in Dublin when she got pregnant. As I understand it, St. Patrick's made my mother give them those details.

This was the first indication of my mother's age when I was born. Before this, Megan and I had been thinking that she'd been in her teens when she became pregnant, so now we worried that she might not still be alive. But what if she were? If we found her, hallelujah! And now our concerns would revert to the ones we'd had since we began this search: Would she accept me? If I had siblings, would they? How would her husband react? I visualized so many possibilities, and most of them scared me.

My father's name was blacked out in the letter. It said only that he had been a thirty-year-old carpenter from County Galway who'd been working in Dublin when I was conceived and that he knew nothing of the pregnancy. I was fine not knowing my father's name. In fact, except for that moment at the psychic's office, I hadn't given him any thought. I'd never *longed* for him.

My (Megan's) Anxiety

Marie wasn't the only one who was nervous about our trip. I couldn't shake the thought of all those stories about children who find their birth families only to learn that those families want nothing to do with them, or their mother has died. Like Marie, I was terrified and tried to psychologically prepare for the worst.

Every night for the two weeks before the trip, the few hours my mind permitted me to sleep were fraught with nightmares of those scenarios and more, including finding Marie's mom with no memory of her first child, or finding that she had passed away the very day before we showed up. I'd wake in a panic, dripping sweat.

My fear of the worst affected how I planned the trip. I built in a tour of the coast, a surprise visit by Mary's family, and other attempts to distract Marie from any disappointments we'd meet.

Pursuing the Dream

In six years, finding Marie's mother (my grandmother) had gone from a dream sealed inside Marie's heart to something shared with hundreds of friends, relatives, and strangers alike. The strangers who became friends—along with Marie's DNA—provided clues, answers, encouragement, and hope.

Now the time had come for us to follow up on Irish soil. As

weeks dissolved into days, hours, and even minutes before our flight, we were both excited and anxious. What would this trip bring? We didn't dare to expect the best-case scenario, but we certainly hoped we wouldn't regret getting on the plane in the first place.

CHAPTER 6

ANGELS AND MIRACLES

New bonds, even with people who were no relation to us, and a series of improbable coincidences led Marie and me on an international search for her mother.

On Sunday, August 27, 2017, we boarded an overnight flight to Dublin. We tried to eat and sleep, but we were still too anxious. So we chatted about, among other things, lowering expectations and defining an acceptable outcome. Once we'd found out that Anastasia was so much older than we had imagined, we no longer assumed she'd be alive and well. So my updated hope was that Marie would be able to meet a cousin, if not a sibling, while Marie said she would just love a picture of her mother so she could see if they looked alike.

That lowered-expectations strategy relieved only some of our tension. Wanting to lighten the mood for both of us, I said that we couldn't let down all the Facebook friends who were following our journey. So if we couldn't find Marie's mother, I proposed a plan B to visit a nursing home, take pictures with some random resident who looks kind of like Marie, and tell everyone we found her. If we ran out of time, we'd just find someone on the streets of Dublin.

Of course, I was only joking, and we had a good laugh. We kept talking throughout the night, unfortunately for the people trying to sleep around us! At some point, my anxiety shifted. I had planned to do all the driving in Ireland myself, but I started to panic at the thought of driving on the "wrong" side of all those narrow Irish roads. I broke the news to Marie, "There's something else that's been bothering me. I'm sorry, but I don't think I can drive over there."

Of course, Marie, being Marie, said, "Don't worry about it; we'll figure it out." I canceled the rental car as soon as we landed. I would ask for a driver at the hotel.

A Brief Complication

Bridie, the desk clerk at our hotel in the center of Dublin, shot that idea right down: "I'm sorry, dear. There's no way I can get you a transport on such short notice. They're all booked up. Maybe we can find you someone in a few days." That won't work, I told her, because we could only *stay* for a few days—five days total to spend in Ireland. I pleaded, "Please call whoever you can, and I'll pay whatever they want."

When I also told Bridie the reason we had come, her eyes got big, and she was instantly on board. She said, "You know what? I have somebody in mind. Go freshen up while I give him a call." We came out of the bathroom just in time to hear, in the exchange amplified by speakerphone, a man's protest: "But it's my day off!"

Bridie replied, "I have these two ladies here. One of them was adopted, and they're looking for her birth mother." As usual, our story galvanized anyone who heard it. After only a brief pause, the man said, "I'll be there in an hour."

Matt McDonald, our driver, was as good as his word. Soon he was ushering us into his car. "Okay, ladies, where are we headed?"

"Two towns about an hour and a half away. One is called Blessington—"

There he broke in, "You're taking me home, are ya?"

Seriously? Of all the towns he could've been from, it was *that* one? What were the odds?

As soon as we told him the whole story, Matt offered us more than transportation. He asked if he could share our mission with some people he knew. Well, *of course.* The first person he called told him, "Sorry, Matt. I don't know anybody by that name, but here's who you should call." So he did, and they referred him to someone else, who referred him to someone else. This went on for a few more calls before he said, "I'm going to call my buddy, John Lennon."

Marie and I exchanged a quick look, while I whispered, "This guy's fucking with us, Mom. He's *not* calling a dead former Beatle."

There was nothing wrong with "this guy's" hearing. Smiling, Matt turned around and said, "I swear to God, that's his real name. Great guy, too—I play music with him in the pubs. He lives near Kiltegan, and he might know somebody."

John Lennon, in turn, offered to call Seamus Doyle, the local historian, who was likely to know more. When Seamus didn't answer, John told Matt that he would head over to Seamus's house. "There's no point in your driving anywhere yet," he advised Matt. "Why don't you take the ladies back to the hotel and email me copies of their notes? We'll go over them tonight."

During that ride, we were blessed with even more material to share with the guys. It came in the form of a message from Claire Sullivan. We met Claire after she saw Marie's blog and contacted Mick to offer her expertise as a Dublin-based genealogist. Today's message said, "After a friend canceled our lunch date, I decided to go to the local GRO (the records office). Here's what I found." She sent us pictures of the birth certificates of Marie's mother and all of her siblings!

Once again, Marie and I were both amazed and grateful that so many people were willing to help random Americans. We still could not have guessed at the time just how much help they had in store for us.

Relative Miracle #1

I'd planned a surprise for Marie that first night. Mary's family, who live on the west coast of Ireland, came to take us out to dinner. We were having a great time when I saw a missed local call on my phone. I picked up a voicemail from John and Matt: "Megan, we've got the whole of Ireland looking for your nana, and we have news. Call us back."

I'll say they had news, which they prefaced with, "Are you sitting down?" Actually, I was leaning against the building because I was a little tipsy. I still hadn't eaten much, and Irish people have a habit of keeping your glass filled. So I said, "No. Do I need to be?"

"You do," John told me, "because my wife, Mary, and Marie are second cousins!"

He went on, "As soon as Matt handed me Marie's picture (as a toddler), I said she looks a lot like my wife at the same age." Then he found the documentation of their blood relation by going through the genealogy and the family tree that Mick sent with us.

Not bad for the first day of our trip, and all because I'd canceled my car reservation. Of course, Marie contends that even if I hadn't, the angels might have had to work a little harder to help us, but they would have found a way.

Then John said, "Cancel the rest of your hotel reservation and stay with us while we keep working on this for you." All of this was based on only a phone call; see what we mean about Irish hospitality?

Not having been born in Ireland, though, I was thinking, "We're supposed to stay with strangers?" But we were in Ireland now, so I quickly got over my misgivings. Marie and I accepted John's generous invitation.

After still another sleepless night for Marie and me, hugely excited, we boarded a bus to Kiltegan. For the entire ninety-seven-minute ride, she stayed silent—seemingly without emotion—while she looked out the window. Later she told me that she'd been in a daze of disbelief during that ride, thinking, "Is this really happening? I don't want to get my hopes up, but this is starting to feel really good."

Everything was happening so fast. Waiting for us at the bus stop on a country road were two smiling faces, those of John and Seamus warmly welcoming us to Kiltegan.

Relative Miracle #2

One of the first things John said to Marie was, "We don't know where your mum is or whether she's alive. But we do know this: Seamus's wife, Betty, and Marie are first cousins. Betty's and Marie's mums are *sisters.*"

Sisters! Things just kept getting better and better. Considering that Marie had come to Ireland just hoping to see a picture of her mother, we were both shocked and grateful at the bounty that these good people were sharing with us. A second cousin and now a first cousin—they were welcoming us into their *family*.

We arrived at the Lennons' beautiful home in the foothills of the Wicklow Mountains. After we met their daughter (who looks a bit like me, by the way) and got settled in, Seamus and Betty showed up, and with more amazing news: they knew the locations of the house where Anastasia had lived until she moved to Dublin when she was twenty, the school she'd dropped out of in the sixth grade, and the cemetery where her father, Patrick O'Leary, is buried. John said, "Tomorrow I'll take you to those places."

Marie, as she has said in this book, is never one to express her emotions too freely, but not even now? I kept looking at her, expecting tears or *something* at the thought of seeing where her mother grew up. But she still gave no reaction—not even when John showed her a photo and said, "That's your mum."

She just calmly gazed at the picture for a moment, said, "She's a cutie," and handed it back to John. I was thinking, "You told me before our plane landed that all you wanted was a photo of your mother. Why isn't this enough to make you burst into tears?"

When I asked her about it later, Marie's response was, "I was confused because the woman in the photo was posing with a giant check—apparently, she had won the lottery—and it covered most of her. What also threw me off was the name on the check, Ann Kelly. A different last name seemed likely, but not the first.

"And the lady in the photo looked nothing like how I envisioned my mother so many years ago. Even at sixty-two years old, I still expected my mom to look like Kathy Miller's mom. Nor did that lady or Betty, for that matter, look like *me*. So I thought, 'I must not have heard him correctly; that can't be my mother.'"

I got a different impression from the photo. I thought, "Oh, no!

Now these sweet people will think we've come after her money!" Of course, we hadn't known about the lottery; we hadn't even known her *name*. But American skepticism dies hard, even in the face of the extreme kindness we were being shown.

I did not need to worry, though. From the moment our relatives met us, they treated us as though we had the best of intentions, which of course we did have.

John and his guitar serenaded us after dinner. Then the family wished us a good night—still another one in which Marie and I were too excited to sleep. In case you haven't been keeping track, we had not slept well in at least a week. It wouldn't be until four days later that we finally chilled out enough to really rest. In fact, the excitement kept building because, even if Marie did not believe she had seen a photo of her mother, now we knew one of her first cousins!

Following Anastasia's Footsteps

After breakfast the following day, John and Seamus took us to the house where Marie's mother and her thirteen siblings were raised. It was hard to believe that all those people fit into a two-room cottage. We learned they were so poor that they couldn't afford enough shoes to go around. The kids would take turns wearing the ones they had; on alternate days, they would have to go barefoot to school, the second stop on our tour.

Then we visited the grave of Anastasia's father, Patrick, in a small cemetery—only about fifty sites—that was meticulously cared for. It was on a hillside with a beautiful view. Flowers, candles, and keepsakes decorated most of the stones, though not his. It touched us to see his name and that of his wife, Bridget, carved next to his. But she wasn't buried there. We wouldn't learn why until the next day.

Marie and I were beginning to feel the essence of the woman who called herself Ann Kelly.

After that family history tour, John drove us through the breathtaking Wicklow Mountains, a thrill for us fans of the movie *P.S. I Love You*! It turned out he had an ulterior motive for extending our drive: he didn't tell us that he was waiting for a phone call.

The call came as we were finishing lunch. Returning to the table, John revealed his hand. Betty had told him that if anyone knew anything about Ann and her secrets, it would be Marie's other first cousin, also named Marie, because the mothers of the two Maries, Ann and Katie, were not only sisters but best friends. "I just heard from another of your first cousins," he told my mom. "She's the daughter of your Aunt Katie, and she lives about fifteen minutes up the road. She said she'd love to meet you. Is now okay?"

Was now *okay*? This is what we had come for!

Relative Miracle #3

(My) Marie will tell the rest:

We rushed to my cousin's house. Thinking like an American, that I'd have to prove my bona fides to someone who would doubt my story, I greeted her with my arms full of paperwork to show I was who I said I was. After I offered them to my cousin Marie, being no American, she gently nudged them away. She said, "I don't need any of that. You look exactly like your mum!"

Hearing those words, I felt like a weight had been lifted from my heart. I'd always hoped that I looked like my mother; the resemblance seemed necessary to confirm that I was a part of her. So I was thrilled to hear my cousin's words. I still didn't cry, though, because at the same time, I also felt a bit dazed—almost as though I was watching these events happening to someone in a movie, not to me. Nothing had fully sunken in yet.

My cousin made us at home in her living room, introduced us to her brother, Paddy, set out tea and sandwiches, and told us about their mother—my aunt, who had passed away only twelve weeks before. And she confirmed the closeness of our mothers. "They spoke on the phone every week until my mother got too sick!"

Then she dropped this bombshell: "If your mom's still alive, she's living in England, and she was alive when I called to tell her about her sister's passing." My mother was alive only three months ago! My cousin let that sink in for a moment before adding, "By the way, you have two half sisters and a half brother there, too."

We had only three days left in the trip, and now we were hearing we'd been looking for my mother in the wrong country! At the same time, though, we wouldn't have skipped even a minute with the lovely people we met in Ireland, even besides the fact that we wouldn't have found her without them.

Why was she in England? Anastasia, then going by Ann, had moved there with her family in 1959, when her husband, a construction laborer, could not find work in Ireland. Her mother moved with her, which solved our mystery of why Bridget is not buried next to her husband, Patrick. Her relocation to England, and the absence of loving keepsakes on his grave, might have had something to do with what we also learned: Patrick was a drunk who verbally abused Bridget and his children.

And just like that, I learned that my mother and I had something in common: being abused as children by an alcoholic and leaving home in search of a better life.

My cousin went into the next room to dial my mother's number, while Megan and I sat waiting on pins and needles. We heard her talking to somebody, but only briefly. As she hung up, we had the same instant fear—that she would tell us, "Someone answered and said Anastasia has just passed away."

Wrong again, thank God! When my cousin returned, she spoke three of the most welcome words I may ever hear, "Your mother answered." Then she said, "She told me she couldn't hear me (she's hard of hearing, you know) and to call back in fifteen minutes when her daughter comes by."

Oh my God. Now I was both dazed and speechless, but in my mind, I was chanting, "She's alive. She's alive."

She's Alive

You've heard the expression, "Time seemed to stand still"? Well, this was one of those moments. What followed were the longest fifteen minutes of my life. My head was spinning while we tried to distract ourselves until Cousin Marie went to fetch us more tea. Megan's and my stress levels were so high at this point that she leaned over to me and whispered, "Oh God, I can't drink another cup of tea. Where's the hard stuff!" I never drink it, but at that moment, I could've used some, too.

When it was time to call back, my cousin went back into the next room and was in there for several minutes before she showed up holding the phone and uttering more welcome words: "Marie, your sister would like to speak to you."

Whoa. I took the phone but couldn't speak. I simply could not believe what was happening. I had to hand the phone to Megan, who put it on speaker while telling my sister, Mary—my sister!—that I was too overcome at the moment. I soon recovered enough to tell Mary what little I knew of Anastasia's premarital background.

Mary said, "I didn't know any of that, but it makes sense. About six months ago, our mam... *your* mam...," she instantly corrected herself. This dear person was already including me in her family! "Our mam had a fever so high that she became delirious and was sobbing hysterically. It was the first time I've ever seen her cry, and I thought, 'Oh my God, she's dying!' It turned out to be only a urinary tract infection, but for the entire night, she screamed, 'They took my baby! *Where's my baby!*'

"By the morning, her fever had subsided, and I asked her, 'Last night, you kept saying that they took your baby. What baby?' She looked at me and said, 'I don't know what you're talking about.' I let the topic drop, but because of that night, when Cousin Marie told me about you, I wasn't surprised."

Thank you, fever! Yet now that I know my lovely relatives, I doubt they would have treated me differently even without the feverish revelation. But it certainly didn't hurt to get her on board so quickly.

Then she said, "Welcome to the family. I can't wait for you to meet everybody." It was clear that she meant it. How incredibly kind she was—*is*. My sister Mary is probably the funniest, sweetest, kindest, and most joyful person I've ever known. She and John's wife, Mary, are the direct opposites of the Mary I'd been forced to grow up with; they changed the whole connotation of that name for me.

The logistics of how to break it to Anastasia still needed to be figured out, and Mary had a plan. "I'll call our brother, Jimmy, and when he gets home from work, we'll go over and tell her that someone—her other daughter—is looking for her. We'll see how that goes and let you know."

Now that we knew my mother was still alive (she's *alive!*), my worry predictably shifted to how she would take the knowledge that I had shown up. I could not forget all those tragic Facebook stories. She could refuse to see me.

I also feared that the shock of even hearing about me would

be too much for her. What if she had a heart attack? It would be all my fault! I was overwhelmed by so many emotions, which also included joy, excitement, and a tiny glimmer of "what if it all goes better than I could have dreamed?"

But if we were going to meet at least my siblings on this trip, we needed to focus on arranging it. Mary told Megan their closest airport, and Megan jumped on booking us a next-day flight to Newcastle, England.

John and Seamus took us back to John's house, where Mary had prepared a delicious dinner. John mentioned, "Do you know what they're doing for you over there in England tonight? They're getting out the good china and polishing the silver." When we said, "We don't want them to go to that much trouble," he replied, "Nonsense—your arrival is not just a special occasion; it's like a national event for this family!"

Matt had joined us, and after the meal, he and John played and sang for us the whole evening. It felt like a pub scene in a movie but better. Before we went to sleep that night, we left our suitcases outside our bedroom door. The next day we found that John had placed on them a poem about the power of the journey; he'd written it before *he* had gone to sleep. All in all, we could not have asked for a warmer welcome or a more wonderful send-off.

Unreal Reality

Megan and I had come *so* far in the three days since we boarded the plane to Dublin that there's not a single doubt in my mind that angels had guided us. To me, there could be no other explanation for Megan's last-minute decision not to drive, our meeting a native son of Blessington and then my second and first cousins, getting to tour my mother's early life, and now this: getting ready for an early flight to meet my mother's family.

It remained to be seen whether we would meet my mother. (I didn't presume to ask too much of the angels!) Because she had kept me and her past a secret throughout the decades, Megan and I knew there was no guarantee, and we certainly didn't want to upset her. But if I could even get a look at her through a window, I decided I would be satisfied—*thrilled*. After all, it was so much more than I'd expected when we began this journey.

CHAPTER 7

FAMILY REUNION

With the big question—"Would she see us?"—preoccupying us, Megan received a Facebook message from my sister Mary the night before we headed to England: "We spoke with her, and she knows you're coming. Come on over; we'll pick you up at the airport." Of course, that answered one question but not the big one, so we called back. Here's what Mary said had transpired when she and Jimmy went over that night:

"'Hey, Mam, there's a woman sitting in Cousin Marie's living room in Ireland right now who says she's your daughter. Did you have a child before you had us?'

"Mam shook her head and said, 'No.'

"Jimmy said, 'We want you to know that whatever happened, we're okay with it. Are you sure you didn't have another one?'

"She paused before admitting, 'Yes, I did.'

"So I said, 'Well, she'll be here first thing in the morning!'

"Mam said, 'Okay then, toodaloo! Off to bed!'"

And with that, she kicked them out of the house. Suddenly it became clear where I got my tendency to keep emotions to myself—it's in the genes.

So now we knew: Ann Kelly—born Anastasia O'Leary, the woman who gave birth to me—would see us! The prayers we didn't even dare to acknowledge had been answered.

Bringing Peace

On the cab ride to the Dublin airport the next day, we met another angel. We had barely pulled away from the bus stop before our lovely driver, Marion Kavanagh, said, "Ah now, ladies, so what's the story?"

Megan reeled it all off for her (she's had a lot of practice!), and then Marion proved that we had gotten into the right car yet again. She pulled off the road to tell us, "I drive this taxi only because I love to talk with tourists about Ireland. But I'm a minister by calling. Do you mind if I pray with you?"

Well, of course, we wouldn't mind! We bowed our heads as she asked God to please grant us a safe journey to my mother. After "amens" all around, this total stranger turned to me and said, "You may think this is your journey, but it's not about you. Your mother needs to find peace, and *this* will bring it to her."

Whether intended for us or not, her words also brought *us* peace. So many amazing things had happened on this trip that by now, you wouldn't think this one would even faze me, but faze me it did. And I was grateful beyond words.

Off to England

We got to the airport, hugged Reverend Kavanagh goodbye, and hopped our flight. Seventy-five minutes later, we landed in Newcastle. That was too soon to prepare me for meeting two of my newfound siblings, who had kindly insisted on picking us up, while I seemed to insist on keeping them waiting.

Megan and I were exhausted after one more sleepless night. More than that, though, I'm sure I've never felt more nervous in my anxiety-filled life. "I need to freshen up," I said as I marched us towards the ladies' room. There I became obsessed with trying to make myself presentable before meeting our relatives.

I've never lost my childhood tendency to sweat profusely when I get nervous, so my hair—uncontrollable even on its best day—had turned into a frizzy mess.

After letting me fuss with it for at least twenty minutes, Megan said, "They're waiting for us; we'd better go." I wrangled my mop into a ponytail and left to face the real source of my nerves—the fear that was another childhood holdover. "What if my family didn't like me? Will they think I'm *ugly*?" My other recurring mental torment was, "What am I doing to my mother and her family by showing up suddenly from out of nowhere?"

I didn't know exactly what we'd be walking into, so while I fought with my hair, I'd been trying to build up my courage.

I had procrastinated so long that when Megan and I finally emerged, ours were the only bags left on the carousel, which had stopped by then. We grabbed them, went outside, and there they were, patiently waiting for us: my sister, Mary, and brother, Jimmy, with his wife, Sammy, and their daughter, Amelia.

With one phone call the day before, the lives of these darling people had changed, yet they greeted us as the long-lost and found relatives they hadn't known they had. First, I was embraced by Jimmy, who was smiling and had tears in his eyes. Then Megan and I went from arms to arms to arms. We fell instantly in love with them all—and, later, with every other relative who showed up to meet us.

Marie and Jimmy's first—teary—embrace.

Mary then joined the consensus of our newly met relatives in Ireland, saying she would have been able to pick me out of a crowd because, "You look just like mam did when she was your age!"

Destination in Focus

On the forty-five-minute drive to our mother's house, Jimmy and Mary shared what they knew of Anastasia's life. After her time in Dublin, she returned to Kiltegan. In 1958 (four years after my birth), she married Michael Kelly, a young man from a neighboring village, on St. Patrick's Day.

(That's still another coincidence: you may recall that my adoptive brother's name was also Michael Kelly, though no relation that we know of.)

Finding no work in Ireland (as Cousin Marie had also told us), the Kellys moved to the English port town of Middlesbrough in 1959. There Anastasia reinvented herself, changing her name to Ann. *That's* why we needed the angels to help us find her!

Jimmy also divulged this bit of more recent history: our mom used to be a secret smoker. He discovered a mound of cigarette butts when he swept her backyard. He never mentioned his find, and after she stopped walking into the village, he would buy a pack and leave a few cigarettes at a time in a plastic bag on the windowsill. She never mentioned them, either. We all amused ourselves by picturing her thanking the leprechauns for bringing them!

As luck would have it, we'd arrived four days before my mother's ninetieth birthday. Megan and I would be able to celebrate it, though a few days early, with my newfound family—sixty-two years after my mother and I had last laid eyes on each other.

Then Mary had this to share: "Just so you know, our Mam has always been the best mother. She did everything for us. We always felt extremely loved, even though she wasn't one to hand out the hugs. Please don't be disappointed if she doesn't embrace you; it's just not who she is."

(Megan's note: Marie and her mom have the first part in common. Marie has also always loved—*treasured*—and done everything for her children, and now her grandchildren. But the two ladies differ in the second part: Marie loves to show her affection with hugs and kisses.)

With Mary's warning, my nerves went into overdrive. The only vision I'd entertained about meeting my mother—wrapping her in a bear hug—had just melted. Now I worried about how I was going to approach her. That worry combined with my recurrent insecurities (would she think that I'm disgusting?) to turn me into even more of a wreck by the time we arrived at the house.

A Meeting of Hearts, Arms, and Hands

When the car reached our destination, it was not as though I rushed into the house. In fact, I froze on the front path, stopping so abruptly that Megan, who was getting her phone ready to video record the reunion, ran right into the back of me. I was overwhelmed by nagging fears: "What am I doing to her? Is she going to like me? How do I approach her?" I said only, "Oh my God, this is *happening*." Gently but insistently pushing me toward the door, she said, "It sure is, and there's no turning back now!"

The door opened, and there stood my beautiful mother! My siblings need not have worried because in addition to the family silver, our mom had brought out the embraces. We locked eyes, walked into each other's arms, sighed at the same time, and didn't let go. The rest of the world had disappeared; suddenly it was just the two of us.

I KNEW YOU WERE THERE

*Meeting my mother for the first time in sixty-two years
could not have been sweeter.*

We grabbed each other's hands and walked to the couch and sat. Then the mother I'd always longed for asked me, "Are you alright?" I said, "I am." When I asked her the same question, she spoke the very same response I'd given to my friend when my third child was placed in my arms: "I am *now*."

As my mother uttered the very words I needed to hear, the waterworks Megan had been expecting for days finally arrived: I burst into tears, followed by every other relative in the room (well, my mother—the most stoic one there—just teared up a little). Now my family was truly complete.

At this point, kind Jimmy gathered the rest of the family (including Megan, my sister Kathleen and her daughter Ava, and Mary's son Michael), and said, "These two need to be alone; let's take a walk to Mary's home." I was grateful, though surprised. They had just met me, and they were leaving this stranger alone with their beloved mother. But they knew she was mine, too.

Just before they left, Mary called me into the kitchen; she and the rest of the family wanted *details*: "Find out who the guy was and everything else you can!" I said, "I don't know that I can do that to her, but I'll try." And Megan set her phone on the mantle to video record our conversation.

They left us holding hands, and I asked her a few questions, beginning with, "Do you remember having me?" She did remember.

Then I asked what I most cared about knowing: "Did you want me to stay with you?" "*Oh, yes,*" my dear mother replied, "of course I did. But they told me I couldn't keep you." About *this* she had more to say: "Two weeks after you were born, a lady came and stole you from me and told me I had to leave St. Patrick's. I didn't know what to do. I had no means, and I didn't know how to find you. All I could do was pray that you were safe. I've kept you in my heart all these years."

Those words—along with the miracle of being able to see her face and hold her hand—were everything I could have wished for. They were everything I needed.

Then, for Mary, I asked, "Do you remember who my father was?" She simply said, "No, I don't," and the steely look in her eyes told me not to press her; she wouldn't go there. (Because she'd named me Maria Goretti O'Leary, my first and middle name for the patron saint of abused children and rape victims, I've often thought that I might have been the product of an assault.)

Now my mother had an important question for me: "Did the people who adopted you treat you well?"

"They did," I said, the first and only lie I would ever tell her. She didn't need to know that truth. I didn't elaborate, and she didn't pursue that line of questioning.

She wanted to know what I do for a living. I told her I'm a nurse working with elderly people, "but for thirty-five years, I took care of babies." She enjoyed hearing that, saying, "I love babies! If I had my life to do over, I would do that, too!"

I told her how beautiful her hair is, and she said, "I had to have that done. I wanted to look good for you." She also wore a dress, which was unusual for the lady, who always wears trousers, Jimmy said.

The Family Returns, Then Celebrates

When everyone came back an hour later, they found us sitting in the exact position they'd left us in: still holding hands and gazing into each other's eyes. We needed to soak each other in, and we did just that. Outside of nights spent at our hotel, we barely let go of each other for the remainder of the visit. (My sister Mary had kindly invited us to stay at her place, but we wanted to give the family and ourselves time and space to process events and decompress.)

It felt so natural to hold on tightly to each other.

I had to confess to Mary that I hadn't gleaned any of the information she was looking for about who my birth father was. She was disappointed but understood. Neither of us wanted to make our mother uncomfortable.

A small gesture meant a lot.

We spent some time perusing old photos of our mother, and sure enough, in these she looked like Kathy Miller's mom and me.

Jimmy then said, "Let's give Mam a little rest. We'll drive you to your hotel to relax, and in a couple of hours, we'll pick you up and take you out to a lovely dinner to celebrate her ninetieth birthday."

A lovely dinner it was, too. Everyone was there: my siblings, including my other sister, Kathleen, and their children and significant others. It felt as cozy and companionable as a Thanksgiving meal with everyone you love around you.

I sat next to my mother, who ordered bangers and mash (thick sausage and potatoes, in case you, like me, had never heard of this traditional UK dish). I instinctively grabbed a knife and fork and started cutting it up for her. Then, on the pretense of going to the restroom, I stopped the waiter and said, "It's going to be my mom's birthday next week. Can I get her a cheesecake with a candle?" (I'd learned it's her favorite cake.) They brought it out at the appropriate time, and everyone sang to her. These were the first things I'd been able to do for my mother, and they felt good, though insufficient.

"We Found Her!"

After an evening that was perfect in every possible way, we returned to our hotel. I was drained and exhausted from all the unaccustomed emotions of the day, not to mention our series of sleepless nights.

But I was still too overwhelmed to sleep. So was Megan, who went to connect some more with her new cousins in the hotel bar. I turned to my phone and opened Facebook where it turned out that throughout the day, Megan had posted updates, along with a photo of our reunion.

My emotions weren't finished with me yet because waiting on my phone were—holy moly—*five hundred* responses. They included Mick, who'd advised me and helped me build my family tree, now in tears of joy at the news; Paul, my crib mate at St. Patrick's Home, who'd also come to my assistance; and Claire Sullivan. She wrote, "My husband thinks I'm having an affair because I've been watching my phone so much today!"

(The night before we returned to the States, we would get together with Claire in Dublin and learn her story. She's another product of a mother and baby home who later found her mother.

But her mother wanted nothing to do with her. Claire's pain and sadness inspired her to use her skills to help reunite many other families. She was thrilled for us.)

Respondents also included friends who sent their love and joined the chorus of, "Oh, my God, Megan. They look so much alike!"

I was stunned; everything had just happened, and now I got to experience it all over again. As I read, I was overwhelmed with gratitude and happiness, and for the second time that day, bawling my eyes out. Then, finally, the exhaustion took over and I—and later Megan, who'd been reading the same Facebook responses in the bar—got some sleep, but probably no more than five hours.

Like Mother, Like Daughter

In the two precious days my mother and I got to spend together during this visit, we learned that our similarities extend beyond just our faces:

Wild Irish hair: while my mother was brushing hers, she told me, "It doesn't matter what I do; my hair always looks like this!"

Big hands and feet, which are particularly massive on our small frames: five foot two for her, and just one additional inch for me. We both wear a 10W (wide) shoe.

Hardworking and always in motion: I learned that people have always asked about my mother, as they always have about me, "Does she ever *sit?*" I take a minimum of twenty thousand steps every day. But even beyond my walks for recreation and fitness, as I've mentioned in the book, I've never been one to sit still. In fact, Megan and I are writing most of this book while I pace, fold laundry, or—my favorite activity—feed my adorable grandson, Megan and Connor's first child, Landyn.

Jimmy and Mary told us that as they and our sister Kathleen got old enough to go to school, our mother would clean two doctors' offices to help make ends meet. She never learned to drive, and she was well known in the village for *scurrying*, not walking, between the offices and back home to care for her children. "There goes Mrs. Kelly!" the villagers were fond of saying. And even at age ninety, my mother still had a spring in her step.

Although I do drive, I, like my mom, took extra jobs to help support the family, including, as I mentioned, a third job to persuade my husband that we could afford a third child. Of course, there's no way I could have known that my own mother also had had three children with her husband or that my third child would be responsible for reconnecting us!

Hard of hearing: Megan calls me deaf as a doorknob. I wouldn't go quite that far. (*What* did you say?) When Mom and I met, she had recently lost her hearing aids, so we all had to speak up a lot. Jimmy and Mary soon replaced them with high-powered ones, so she would be able to hear phone calls from me.

Our similarities also extend beyond the physical, lending proof of the strength of nature over nurture:

Outdoor clotheslines: my mother and I bonded again in her backyard when we shared our love for sheets that smell fresh after they hang in the breeze. She still used a clothesline with wooden clothespins; I gave up mine when my kids were grown.

Born to nurture: Megan affectionately calls my mother a "tea pusher." Mom has always wanted people to feel at home by placing a steaming cup in front of them. "Ah, let's get ya a cup of tea." ("But I'm already *drinking* a cup of tea!")

Once Mary went to check on her "and sitting at her table, the mailman was drinking tea and eating a sandwich. When he left, I said, 'Mam, you can't be inviting people into the house when you're here alone!' 'But the poor fella was famished!'"

And she had tried to feed me the entire time the family had

left us alone, but I said, "Thank you; I just can't eat right now."
When they returned, she complained first to Mary, then to Jimmy,
"She won't eat or drink anything!" Each in turn said, "It's okay;
she's pretty excited about meeting you."

I don't push tea and food, but I became a nurse because I
enjoy being of service.

We adore babies, and children in general: my heart melts every
time I see a child. As Mom had just told me, hers melts, too. She
would ask to pick up every baby that came her way. Knowing her
strong love for children makes it all the more devastating that her
first child was stolen from her.

A tendency to spend money only on others: my mother used
the 200,000 pounds she won in the English lottery to pay off
her three kids' mortgages. I would have done the same. And
like her, I never save even a penny or spend one on myself.
(For me, not saving probably has to do with my experience
with my adoptive mother. If I ever left money lying around,
she would grab it.)

Preference for Bailey's Irish Cream: Neither Mom nor I really
drink, but for special occasions, it's our go-to, unless it's a shandy
(beer and lemonade), which she drank at her birthday dinner.

Peace with the Catholic Church: my mother went to Sunday
Mass, and her children made their first communion and got
married in the Catholic Church. So she either didn't blame the
church for what had happened to her or she had forgiven it.

You might think that my rosary ordeal would have turned
me off to the church forever, but the music, the kind nuns who
taught me, and the growing thought that angels were guiding me
brought me back. I wanted my children to have the connection,
so Jack and I took them to church and enrolled them in a small,
family-oriented Catholic school.

Two Irish Hearts and a
Cleveland Connection

Before Jimmy dropped us off at the hotel that night, I asked if he would drive us in the morning to a shopping area. I'm no shopper, but I wanted to find a special birthday present for my mother. He said, "You're already in the city center; Mary, Michael, and I will just meet you and Megan in your hotel's lobby, and we can stroll to the shops."

The five of us had walked for only a few minutes when Megan spotted, at the top of a building, a huge sign that read, "CLEVELAND." What was *that* about? Jimmy explained that we were in none other than *Cleveland* (city) Centre. No way! We had found my mother by traveling from Cleveland, Ohio, in the US, to Cleveland, Middlesbrough, in England. (All this time, the angels had tried to send us an obvious clue for our research, but we'd totally missed it!)

After walking for a few minutes, we came to a quaint gift shop, and something led me to the back of the store. There was a dainty silver necklace with two hearts—one inside the other. It represented me and my mom and how we had kept each other in our hearts. We had said those very words to each other when we met. It felt like the perfect gift.

Later that afternoon, I presented Mom with it, and you could tell she loved it. She kept touching it after Jimmy placed it around her neck. He did the honors because my hands were shaking too much to work the clasp! I was thinking, "I never got to give my mother a gift before; this is her ninetieth birthday, and I'm giving her a gift, just as any daughter would." Once again, I was overwhelmed with gratitude that I was granted this experience.

The first gift I was ever able to give my mother was for her soon-to-come ninetieth birthday.

Later, except for when she went out for dinner, she kept the necklace hanging on her mantle where she could see it from her "throne," as the family called her favorite chair. She said she was afraid that if she wore it all the time, she would lose it.

In addition to all the priceless gifts I'd received on this trip, on the day we left, I also received tangible ones.

Let me set the stage for the presentation: my mother and I had a day and a half of soaking each other in, and the thought of leaving my mother devastated me. My thoughts ran to, "Am I ever going to see you again? Oh, God, even if this must be *it,* I'll always remain grateful for every single thing that happened here."

My mother also had tangible gifts for me, including this rosary.

So when my mother held out a small box, saying, "Here are some things to remember me by" (as if I wouldn't!), I felt my heart breaking. The box contained an Irish rosary, a pen silkscreened with the word "Ireland," and a little shamrock keychain that she'd probably taken with her from her native country so many years before. They meant everything to me. For the third time during that trip, my tears came.

My three wonderful siblings also gave me a treasure in addition to welcoming me and Megan into their family with wide-open arms. They presented me with a canvas tote bag printed with "Sisters are the best!" I was so touched.

Toodaloo We Meet Again

The next day, Megan and I had to say goodbye to my mother—one of the hardest things we've ever done. It broke our hearts to leave her and we would leave a piece of them in Cleveland, England. After leaving us with a hug and one of her favorite sayings, "God is good," she went to the window and waved. "That's what she always does for her kids and grandkids," said Jimmy. "She's sending you off with a smile, a hug, and a wave, to make sure you're safe." That image and those words triggered the fourth flood of tears from me, along with more tears from Megan, as much as we struggled to hold them back.

But although it was gut-wrenching to have to say goodbye, my mother's enthusiasm and physical energy gave Megan and me hope that we would see her again. We prayed for it. In the meantime, we consoled ourselves with the fact that she was being loved and cared for. My siblings and their children doted on her, called her "The Queen," and treated her like one, as she deserved.

In turn, my siblings' goodness reflected how much our mother had always loved and cherished them. In addition to enormous gratitude to have touched her and devastation to have to leave

My mother wishes us farewell where, we later learned, she always waves to her departing family members.

her, I couldn't help but feel sad that I didn't grow up with them. But my life had not been destined to go that way.

On the ride back to the airport, sweet Jimmy kept the conversation light. He joked, "I wonder what other secrets Mam's been hiding from us! Don't worry; if there are any more, Mary will ferret them out!" Then he mentioned his surprise that our mother had dressed up so much—in a skirt the first day of the visit and a "frock" the second. She wore a fuzzy coat out to lunch with us on that second day, causing him to affectionately tease her, "Mam, you look like a Goddamn polar bear!"

Jimmy also talked about how much fun we'd all had during the visit and how happy they all were to have another sister and more nieces and a nephew. When we said goodbye, he whispered, "I love you." Even writing those words makes me tear up.

We had experienced many miracles and blessings in two short days. We'd gone from the welcome news that my mother would see us, to actually getting to see, touch, and fall in love with her and my adorable "new" family members, in Cleveland of all places. Nothing could have meant more to me.

Of all the extreme emotions fighting for attention inside of me (and which would take me months to process), it was gratitude that won.

Living the Dream, Embracing the Journey

At the Cleveland (Ohio) airport, about to embark on our journey, we were both hopeful and terrified.

When we arrive in Dublin, we enjoy a visit with the family of my adoptive mother.

Meeting my first cousin, Mary Lennon (John's wife).

Megan and her second cousin, Natalie, discover a remarkable family resemblance.

We visit the two-room cottage where Anastasia and her thirteen siblings grew up.

Lunch with John Lennon and Seamus Doyle in Ireland's stunning Wicklow Mountains during our tour of Anastasia's childhood environment.

The family in Ireland waits for Ann's call.

With John Lennon and Matt McDonald at John's house.

Meeting my sister Mary.

Ann, born Anastasia, with all of her children.

Surrounded by love.

Megan meets her cousins.

Living in the same city (name) but on different continents!

Adoring profiles.

The queen on her throne.

Out on the town.

We never let go of each other for the entire trip.

On the ride to a special evening out.

Our family is together to celebrate Ann's ninetieth birthday.

What joy looks like.

*In Dublin, we meet Claire Sullivan, the genealogist who kindly
supplied us with essential research.*

*Before flying home, we travel to Edinburgh to meet Mick McNulty—
the gracious mastermind of our journey.*

CHAPTER 8

WE MEET
AGAIN, JUST
IN TIME

Our mother was eager to keep in touch with me. Mary said, "She keeps telling people, 'I've got a new phone and hearing aids now so I can talk to my daughter in America!'" Before she confessed her decades-old secret to her three other children, the only person she'd told was her sister, Katie, who took it with her to her grave. But now that it was out, it was *really* out; she was *proud* to talk about me.

About once a week, I would give her a call, and these calls almost always went the same precious and abrupt way—none more than a minute. Every time she heard, "Mam, it's Marie," she would say, "Oh, Marie, how are ya, darlin? Are ya all right?" I would say, "I am. I miss you. How are you?" And she'd say, "I'm doing fine, too. Bye bye, toodaloo now!" *Click.*

The first time she basically hung up on me, I was so surprised I just sat there staring at the phone.

I told Mary about that first call's brevity, and she just laughed, saying, "Well, of course! You're one of us, and that's exactly how she talks to us!" That detail brought me indescribable joy.

Every now and then on these calls, my mother would throw in, "You know, I'm moving a little slow today." It was about November, a few months after we left, when Mary said, "Mam's starting to fail. Her doctor said that a tumor in her lungs that was inactive is growing." The news struck terror in my heart. Now I was sure I would never see her again.

Megan interceded again: on Christmas morning, she handed me an envelope containing a plane ticket and said, "You're going back to see your mother in early February."

I couldn't believe it! Even my dreams about seeing her again didn't include how I would be able to travel back to England. I couldn't—can *never*—thank Megan enough, and I could hardly wait to be with my mother again.

Finally, February

By the time the six weeks passed and I did see my mother again, the cancer had taken over: she had lost a lot of weight, and she needed pain medication and much more of her local children's help.

Jimmy, Mary, and Kathleen scheduled a consultation with our mother's doctor so they could include me, as their sister. That felt incredible and further cemented our bond as siblings. They had long ago dropped the "half" from the words "half sister."

Even though we probably had a different dad (not that we'll ever know), they had embraced me as their sister, period.

During the meeting in which I learned my mother's gall bladder also plagued her, these lovely people kept turning to me and asking, "What do you think?" I demurred, saying, "I'm just a nurse," while encouraging them to do whatever felt right to them. Ultimately, we all agreed to get on board with whatever would keep her comfortable.

For the five nights of the visit, I slept on a mattress on her living room floor. I took care of her as much as she'd let me, fetching her medication and helping her dress. But she'd insist on making *me* breakfast and tea. At night, I would say good night, hug her, tuck her in bed, and go to my mattress. Five minutes later, I'd hear her footsteps and sweet voice: "Do ya have everything ya need?" Despite her pain, she wanted to make sure I was taken care of.

Somehow, with us both trying to take care of the other, we both got exactly what we needed: an even deeper mother–daughter bond with countless hugs. What a blessing!

During my February visit, we lived together like mother and daughter.

The second night I was there, her medication couldn't relieve her pain, and I couldn't bear to see her suffer. I asked Mary to call an ambulance to take her to the hospital. Maybe they could do something for her.

When Mary got a bit of an argument from the hospital about whether they needed to come out. I told her, "Just force the issue and get them to come so they can help her." They finally agreed to come, but when Mary and I went into the bedroom, our mother was resting quietly. Well, *that* wouldn't do, so we told her to ham it up and moan a little when they showed up, so they would take her to the hospital. She said, "You mean like this? Ohhhhhh."

"Yes, that's perfect!"

Opening night didn't go like the dress rehearsal, though. When the ambulance arrived, our mother sprang into her typical hostess mode: "Have you had anything to eat? Mary, they look famished; get them a cup of tea and a sandwich." Meanwhile, in the background, I was thinking, "No, no, no, *no!*"

But somehow, the EMTs (or whatever they're called in England) agreed to take her to the hospital, where every time a doctor or nurse came in to get her history, she showed more interest in theirs: "I think I've seen you before. Did you get married? Do you have any children?" Not even pain could keep her from being adorable.

After several hours in which they were unable to do anything for her, they sent her home.

Megan and her husband, Connor, had arranged to arrive for the final three days. She wanted more time with her Nana, her aunts, uncle, and cousins, and she wanted Connor to meet them all. Of course, her Nana wanted that, too, and she fell in love with him. He would sit and talk with her, and she... well, you know, "Get the man something to eat, for God's sake!"

Another family portrait.

A Still More Painful Goodbye

The day arrived when the three of us had to leave her and the rest of our beloved, recently found family. Once again, I hosted an array of emotions. For someone who had grown up stifling them, I can tell you that experiencing so many feelings all at once caused me a lot of stress!

I was overjoyed and grateful that I was granted that time with her. In a way, this visit felt even better than the first because we got to live together, like a mother and daughter rather than like a guest and hostess. My siblings came around only when we needed something. They sweetly gave our mother and me plenty of cherished time alone with each other. She filled me up throughout our healing hours and days together. We'd been given the precious opportunity to absorb the essence of each other.

Of course, it also killed my heart to say goodbye. Given her illness, this time I knew for sure that I wouldn't see her again. Sadness flooded me.

I can't say I wallowed in emotions on the flight home from Scotland because I was occupied, along with the bathroom I took refuge in. Bad milk in my hot chocolate at the airport gave me food poisoning. While my physical feelings commanded my attention, I lay on the bathroom floor for five of the seven hours of the flight until I agreed to take an Alka-Seltzer. It was an altogether strange end to a beautiful visit.

"Don't Worry. God Is Good."

Almost as soon as we returned to Ohio, Mom's health went further downhill. Mary would call me every couple of days from our mother's house to keep me informed. They would take turns talking to me.

At some point, our mother could barely eat. Mary called during the first week in April to say, "I don't think she has long now." Then she said, "I'm going to put the phone next to her on speaker, leave the room, and close the door, so you can say your goodbyes, though she probably won't respond. I'll leave you alone for a half hour, and if I hear you still talking when I come to the door, I'll stay away for longer. Take all the time you need."

My three siblings were sitting there watching their beloved mom die, and Mary thought about me! Her loving kindness so overwhelmed and touched me that at first, I could barely speak. But it should not have overwhelmed me because I already knew that's how all three of my siblings are.

I don't claim to have said anything momentous in this final call—just that I prayed she wasn't in pain, I was glad she had her beautiful children with her, and that most of all, she was in my heart. I told her how much I loved her and always would.

I also told her other things, like how happy our physical resemblance makes me, at least when I could speak between my sobs. But I knew she didn't care about the words that didn't come. Then I recalled what she said to Megan, Connor, and me when we left in February: "Don't worry. God is good." Ending the call the same way felt just right.

During the next ten days, whenever I called, the family gathered by her bedside would include me in their conversation as they reminisced about growing up together.

Lost, Found, Gone

On Sunday, April 15, 2018, I was feeling particularly brokenhearted about my mother's illness as I walked into my local Starbucks for my usual morning cup of coffee.

I had become friendly with Gretchen, one of the baristas, who had celebrated the finding of my mother with me and hung on every detail before and after. In one glance, she took in my sadness: "How are you?"

"I don't think it's going to be long," I tearfully told her. "I wish I could be there. I feel so *guilty*." With that, she grabbed my hands, looked me in the eyes, and said, "Marie, you weren't meant to be there now. You were there when she needed you. You brought her peace."

As she spoke those words, the feeling of lead in my chest disappeared. It felt as if my mother was talking through her, telling me, "It's okay. *I'm* okay." I felt, once again, as if I'd been touched by an angel.

I got my drink and hadn't gone more than six steps from the counter when my phone buzzed with Jimmy's text: "Mam has passed."

Megan and I were preparing for the state inspection of her

residential care home, so I would not be able to attend the funeral. My siblings found a way to include me anyway. They called and asked if there was anything I wanted buried with our mother. I did—the very soft blanket (blue-green, the color of her eyes) that I bought her during my February visit on a sisterly shopping trip with Mary, and, of course, the double-hearts necklace.

Someone video recorded the funeral for us, and while the Irish priest eulogized our mother's goodness, her adorable personality, and the amazing family she raised, he said, "She was so wonderful that her daughter in America came over here twenty times (a bit of blarney there) to try to find her."

I was heartsick to lose our mother so soon after I had reconnected with her. But at the same time, I felt enormously blessed and grateful. We *did* reconnect, and she and her family welcomed us.

Blessed by Angels

The story could have ended so differently. In fact, I expected it to. But Megan and I have come to believe that my mother so needed to find peace that she kept herself alive long enough to achieve the absolute best-case scenario. With the help of our angel friends and relatives, we *all* received the gift of a miracle.

My life began in darkness—being stolen from my birth mother and tormented for years by my adoptive one. It took me decades to rid myself of the misconception ingrained in me that I was ugly, disgusting, and worthless.

Of course, things were much worse for my mother; few tragedies feel more profound to a parent than the loss, by any means, of a cherished child.

My mother and I both went on to live fulfilling lives, but we never let go of the longing for each other. That all the angels in my life conspired to bring us together remains the single greatest blessing of my life.

Reconnection in Its Own Good Time

My adoptive mother was never my mother, and I was never her daughter. With my real mother and family, I was finally a daughter, and through becoming one, I became so much more: a sister to three additional precious people, and finally an aunt. In the process, I also came face to face with the truth that I'd believed since I was five years old—and it was better than I could have imagined.

Out of darkness—my living nightmare—came the brightest light; I waited years to see it, but there were always angels, like Mrs. Miller, the mom of my first friend, Kathy Miller, who showed me what a mother could be.

You too have guardian angels that you might find in a cab or a coffee shop or anywhere else. So if you're living a tortured existence, as I was, please don't ever give up. I hope that the story of my life illustrates for you what I learned: no matter how improbable it may seem, you *can* overcome your past—by seeing good in the people around you, by deciding you are not a victim, and by choosing to be better and do better than the people tormenting you.

You can not only find a way out and survive, but, like me, you can thrive. Good people who interceded taught me those lessons. I pray that you have them in your life, too.

Draw on the strength inside you, even though everything seems stacked against you, and try to be patient. Megan and I learned that things happen when they're supposed to, not necessarily when you want them to. It seems clear to us that if we had tried to find my mother at any other time, we would have failed.

And if you're looking for your birth mother or child, I wish you angels on your path. May they help you find the person you've always yearned for and be embraced when you do. But please prepare yourself for any possible outcome. If my mother had rejected me so she could keep her feelings of shame locked in her heart, I was determined to respect her boundaries and go away.

If you don't find the reception you dream of, I pray you'll find peace and other connections as you go about your life. Perhaps you'll be inspired to follow the shining example of Claire Sullivan, who supports the searches of her fellow adoptees.

May your story have a happy ending.

Thank you for your interest in ours.

THE END

I KNEW YOU WERE THERE

RESOURCES

Where to turn if you're struggling with some of the issues we cover in the book:

For protection against child abuse or to report child abuse, contact Childhelp www.childhelp.org or call their National Child Abuse Hotline at 1-800-4-A-CHILD, 1-800-422-4453.

To get help with recovering from alcoholism, contact Alcoholics Anonymous www.alcoholicsanonymous.com or 1-866-972-0134.

If you want to start the search for your own lost loved one, contact www.adopted.com or www.adoptionnetwork.com.

Thrilled to Give Back

We'll donate a portion of the proceeds from this book to Providence House, Inc., a Cleveland, Ohio-based organization that fights child abuse and supports family preservation.

If you also would like to support this worthy cause, please contact www.provhouse.org or 1-216-651-5982.

ACKNOWLEDGMENTS

You know the saying, "It's too good to be true"? Well, that's how we always begin telling people the story of how we found Marie's mother. We say we know it sounds that way, and we don't even know if we would believe it if we hadn't seen it all unfold with our own eyes. We truly witnessed a miracle.

This miracle could not have come to be if it weren't for all the amazing people who helped us along the way out of the goodness of their hearts. Because of you all, my mother and hers were given peace. I can't think of two more deserving people to get to live the miracle of a lifetime, but without all our angels, it never would have happened. Our family is eternally grateful.